Praise for

"Gripping, poignant, and ins̲ ̲ ̲ ̲ ̲ ̲ ̲ ̲how pride can help to power through suffering and create meaning. Author Catherine Ehrlich, drawing heavily on vivid memoirs written by her grandmother, has added depth of research, beauty of language, and a haunting present-day perspective to the life of an extraordinary woman of Vienna during wartime and beyond."
—Dori Jones Yang, author of *When the Red Gates Opened: A Memoir of China's Reawakening*

"This beautifully written combination of a Holocaust survivor's memoir with the recollections and research of her grand-daughter captures the charms of fin-de-siècle Bohemia and the devastation that followed. Imaginative, compelling, clear, and touching, the narrative of an emancipated and educated woman's heartbreak during the First World War, new love and hope in 1920s Vienna, despair again as the Nazis closed in, and escape with her only son to America illustrates the human cost of intolerant and violent politics in Central Europe. *Irma's Passport*, a new addition to the vast literature on fascism and anti-Semitism, deserves attention from readers of all ages."
—Jeremy King, Professor of History, Mt. Holyoke College

"A gripping and well-written story about a courageous woman living between the world wars. Irma is a spitfire of a woman who attended university when there were only 4 percent women students, and who shared an English literature class with Franz Kafka—historical figures pop out like gifts in the story. The book also provides a window into the assimilated life of the Jews of Bohemia, early Zionism, Antisemtism, and the Holocaust. Your foreknowledge prepares you for what is coming but, inspired by Irma, you hold your breath and read on."
—Leora Krygier, author of *Do Not Disclose: A Memoir of Family Secrets Lost and Found*

Irma's Passport

Irma's Passport

*One Woman,
Two World Wars,
and a Legacy
of Courage*

CATHERINE EHRLICH

SHE WRITES PRESS

Published 2021
Printed in the United States of America
Print ISBN: 978-1-64742-305-6
E-ISBN: 978-1-64742-306-3
Library of Congress Control Number: 2021907686

For information, address:
She Writes Press
1569 Solano Ave #546
Berkeley, CA 94707

Interior design by Tabitha Lahr

She Writes Press is a division of SparkPoint Studio, LLC.

Contents

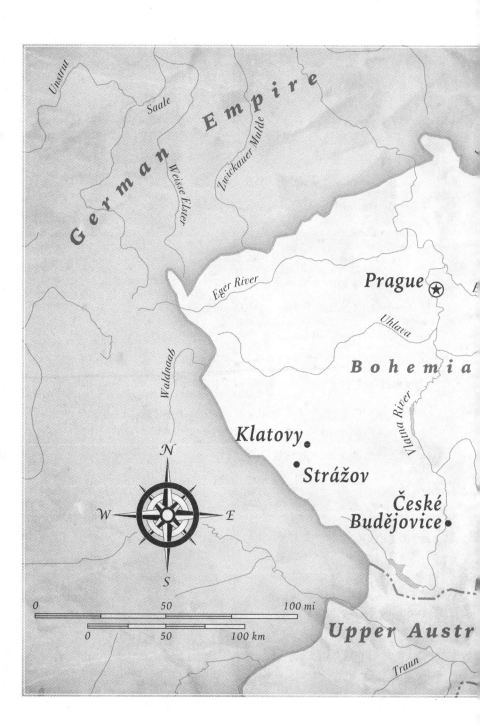

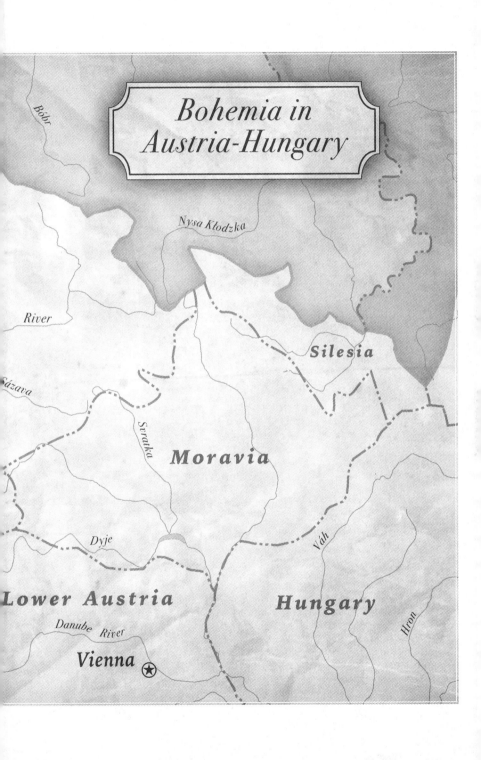

Bohemia in
Austria-Hungary

Bóbr

Nysa Kłodzka

River

Sázava

Silesia

Svratka

Moravia

Dyje

Váh

Lower Austria

Hungary

Danube River

Hron

Vienna ⊛

Singer Family

many generations in Bohemia

Moritz Singer b 1838
*m*1 Marie Lasner b 1825
*m*2 Julia Kohner b 1843

Rudolph b 1857
m Marx
one son
descendants in USA

Julius b 1867
m Singer
two sons
descendants in Israel

Karoline b 1868
m Hütter
four daughters
descendants in USA

Louise b 1869
m Epstein
one son, one daughter
descendants in USA

Siegmund b 1870
m Schoenfeld

Josefine b 1874
m Sinek
two daughters

Emil b 1878
m Kohn
two daughters

Hütter Family

many generations in Bohemia

Johann Hütter b 1861
m Karoline (Karla) Singer b 1868

Irma b 1890
*m*1 Erwin Kolmar b 1886
  *m*2 Jakob Ehrlich b 1877

Mela b 1892
m Otto Brok b 1876
two sons

Edna b 1894
m Friedrich Werner b 1881

Hedi b 1898

Paul Ehrlich b 1923
m Celia Lesley b 1926
three sons, two daughters
including the author
descendants in USA

Lily b 1921
m Heinrich Schaefer
two sons
descendants in Brazil

Hans b 1924

Hannah b 1924
m Isaak Braun
one son, one daughter
descendants in Israel

*Irma and Catherine share-wear Irma's Austrian folk
ensemble with edelweiss trim, early 1970s*

Prologue

Irma and I

———◆———◆———

My grandmother, Irma Ehrlich, was nearly eighty-two years old in 1971 when she flew from Manhattan to join me in Hokkaido, the northernmost island in Japan, where I was living as a seventeen-year-old exchange student in the Buddhist temple compound of my host, Ryuei Hata.

Irma sat in the one Western-style chair in Hata's tatami sitting room, her sturdy calves crossed and her dandelion puff of hair pale in the dimming light. Hata and I gathered nearby on floor cushions beside the wide window overlooking Ishikari Bay. Nightjars scythed through the sky after insects as we gazed over blue and red rooftops to the harbor below, watching the last ferryboat glide in like a glowing caterpillar from forbidden Vladivostok.

Vladivostok, Irma was saying, was where her brother-in-law, Fritz Werner, was imprisoned when he was captured just four months after the start of the Great War in 1914. He'd survived on packages delivered by the Red Cross and kept up hope by learning languages from fellow prisoners. After the war ended in 1918, it took him four years to wend his way back overland to a newly minted country called Czechoslovakia. When he knocked at his front door after nearly eight years of bitter hardship, his wife, Irma's sister, couldn't recognize him at first. Irma paused. "The nine languages Fritz practiced in prison became his passport to a good job in business," she concluded.

Hata rolled back on his cushion with the audible air intake that is Japanese for amazement. The dignified woman in his guest chair was older and stronger and worldlier than anyone in his Pure Land Buddhist congregation, and she brought faraway empires right into his home. As for me, I'd always known Irma as old and strong and spellbinding. A prompt like "Vladivostok"— locked behind the Iron Curtain—was sure to bring forth tales of miraculous escapes, of families reunited, and of great wealth lost and restored. Her stories often seemed to say "Don't lapse into victimhood; use languages as your passport to the world," and I had absorbed the lesson. I'd spent countless hours after school studying Japanese while feeling captive as a restless teen in Buffalo, New York, before winning the Rotary Club scholarship to live abroad. Without my knowledge, Irma paid for my flight to Japan.

In my childhood I believed my grandma's promise that she would put me in her suitcase and take me abroad. I imagined myself curled up like a kitten, keeping silent to avoid capture. We shared the secret bond that exists between redheads: something rare, aligned, unspoken. Her example planted in me the notion that a woman could achieve mastery in foreign languages and belong wherever she lived. In Japan, I believed that my fluent Japanese and immersion in the country could make me Japanese, and like her I didn't conceive of race or religion as a barrier to belonging.

She knew eight languages—Czech, German, French, Italian, English, Latin, a little Hebrew, and some Turkish. She'd attended Charles University in Prague in 1910 as one of its first female students, crossed Alpine glaciers in ankle-length leather skirts in the 1920s, and rebuilt her life after two devastating European wars.

Language mastery and indomitability had carried her through. I thought of her as unembittered, unbowed, victorious.

When she was my age she was a milky-skinned, golden-haired girl in a storybook place called Bohemia, dreaming of a larger stage for her life. In her early eighties she flew halfway around the world to join me and climb the 1,368 steps of Konpira-san shrine while Japanese pilgrims half her age labored haltingly. We inhaled the scents of azaleas and wet moss at golden Kinkaku Temple and marveled at ancient ink scrolls. Irma and I floated in pale blue mist in a light blue boat across deep blue Lake Hakone, joking about feeling bluish. Bluish, a sort of color, a play on being sort of Jewish. I never felt Jewish. That part of my heritage belonged mostly to the past, I thought, in those bygone places like Austria-Hungary and Bohemia. I loved to hear her memories of exotic times and places, though I struggled to keep her stories straight. Someday, she said, she would retire from her job at a law office in New York and write her memoirs.

Luck had placed me in a Buddhist compound at a time when young Americans were probing Eastern philosophies for truth. I had been raised by two atheists, one raised Jewish and the other Christian, who seemed to think that a founding principle of America was freedom *from* religion. Curious, I pestered Hata for a lesson in Buddhism prior to Irma's visit. One evening he poured himself a large tumbler of Johnny Walker Black on ice and began with the Four Noble Truths: life is suffering; suffering is caused by desire; detach from desire to seek enlightenment, which brings freedom from rebirth and an end to this earthly cycle of suffering.

The essence of life is compassion, Hata said. I didn't believe him. Life was not suffering; it was full of joy and promise. Was he suffering? Was I? Everyone wants more life, so why does Buddhism present reincarnation as some kind of punishment? Hata chuckled at my irreverence, finished his whiskey, and threw up his hands.

On the night before Irma's departure, Hata sat cross-legged on the tatamis like a pupil at the foot of Irma's chair. Speaking slowly, his eyes cast downward, he queried a pillar of his faith: "Buddhism teaches us how to avoid rebirth. If you could choose to live again, would you do it?"

    I knew what my wise and wonderful grandmother would say. Then I watched her head sink and heard the wrong word drop. "No," she said.

....

My shock at her response came back to mind in 2014 when, at the age of sixty, I started to compile her story. Irma began typing her memoirs after she retired at eighty-six and continued past the time she could see. Line overwrote line; passages began twice and headed in different directions. Fragments hinted at lost pages and sentences floated off-margin to tease like poetry. Her only son, my father, Paul, edited and retyped some sections in the years before he died in 2003. Sifting through files to get organized, I found an email response to a question I had asked Paul two years before his death: "So, Cat, it looks like you're turning out to be the family historian!" he wrote, and I ached to live up to the challenge, for both family and history.

    Historical narratives oversimplify by necessity, and the one I grew up with went like this: "World War II is over, the good guys won, and America is a place for loosening past tribal enmities." Like protective parents anywhere, Irma and Paul had opened up about the past gradually, when they thought their offspring safely distant from it. I had a tingling sense of curiosity and wariness toward Germanic and Jewish ancestry, and the Zionism of my visionary grandfather, Jakob Ehrlich. I knew outcomes and punch lines like "not half bad for a start," but lacked answers to the whens and whys. I wanted to nest Irma's stories in their proper historical landscape as things happened, before historical narratives made all seem inevitable, and thereby restore a color picture from the black-and-white fragments I had.

I had Irma's extraordinary firsthand account but a lot of learning to do. My research proved delightful in the way it helped to make sense of episodes from Irma's prodigious memory. She wrote in tantalizing detail about many people yet with big gaps. When famous names like Kafka, Einstein, Freud, and British public figures sprang up, other accounts corroborated hers. To trace her life was to traverse a virtual century of European history, and to place my family within it.

Dozens of books and hundreds of Internet hours along, I noticed the roots of nationalism that had shaken the world and then resprouted in familiar and discomfiting patterns in America, Britain, and Europe. Popular culture—*The Sound of Music*— trivializes the power of tribal bonds, social pressures, nationalistic symbols, fear, and pure force. Parallels between her times and ours—especially the tensions among unity, nationalism, and identity—emerged like red flags. The same questions pertinent to Irma then are the ones I am now asking: Is my nation falling apart along ethnic nationalist lines? Will racial divides undo us? Will a class war erupt? Later on, historians will select the salient trends and present them as inevitable, or at least more predictable than they really are now.

Irma's Passport has emerged as a kind of cross-generational collage: I frame the long view; she provides the close-ups. I let her words flow where I can, marking her passages with a slight indent, and support her in brackets for clarity. Using great care not to change her meaning, I rearrange passages, reconcile versions, and adjust her German syntax. In addition to historical landscape, I supply elements from family lore that she did not write down. Together, Irma and I tell her story.

Irma, Mella, and Edna Hütter, 1895

A Bohemian Fairy Tale

1890

━━━━◆────────■─◆━━━

In the great Empire of Austria, in the province of Bohemia, rows of pastel buildings lined the tidy central square of Klatovy (Klattau), around which eleven thousand Austrian Czechs lived. From one corner of the square the venerable white Jesuit church watched over the town's mostly Catholic souls, while the medieval black watchtower next to it scanned over low houses to a patchwork of barley, sugar beet, and carnation fields. Across the cobblestoned square, past the apothecary shop, and down Prague Street stood the two-story stucco house where my grandmother, Irma Hütter, was born on August 28, 1890, above her father's store.

Irma was the firstborn child of Karoline (Karla) and Johann Hütter. Introduced by a matchmaker, they had fallen in love at first sight and married in 1888 when Karla was twenty and Johann, Hans, or "Witty Hanousek," as she called him, was twenty-seven. She was a handsome woman of burnished auburn hair and intelligent gray eyes, born in Strážov and raised in Klatovy. He, of merry brown eyes and bristly mustache, was the prosperous owner of the town's farm implements and hardware store. After

Irma came her sisters Melanie (Mela, 1892), Edna (1894), and finally Hedwig (Hedi) in 1897.

Klatovy lay along the northwest edge of Austria-Hungary, the third most populous empire after Great Britain and Russia, ruled from Vienna under the Hapsburg crown. The empire consisted of linguistic and ethnic subgroups: 23 percent German, 20 percent Hungarian, 13 percent Czech, and smatterings of Slavic and Italian peoples settled in the traditional homelands. Austria's national religion was Catholicism and the national language German. The Hütter family was bilingual in German and Czech, and Jewish by religion, part of a 2 percent minority in Klatovy and just over 4 percent in the overwhelmingly Catholic— 80 percent—empire.

Today Klatovy's central square looks much as it did in the nineteenth century, with automobiles parked where horse teams and wagons once stood. It lies near the German border in the western part of the Czech Republic, which covers most of the Czech-speaking regions formerly known as Bohemia and Moravia. Irma described her formative years in Bohemia:

I

The house where my parents lived stood at the corner of Prague Street, the main street leading into the cobblestoned town square. The house had a store on the ground floor in the front and living quarters upstairs. In the rear was a storehouse for farm implements and heavy building materials. On market days, a solid line of ox carts stretched from the town square along Prague Street to our house. Peasants awaited their turn to get into the store, which was filled to capacity with people testing the sharpness of scythes, sickles, and other tools. Daddy attended the crowd with two employees helping. Just outside, peasant women spread their wares in the square: eggs, pounds of butter wrapped in cabbage leaves, poultry, berries, fruits, and mushrooms from the forests of the Bohemian woods to the west.

A promenade bordered by trees ran next to the house, sloping down to a lively stream, the Angel. From our street a bridge crossed the Angel to a row of houses and a smithy. I loved to watch the smith with his apron blackened, hammering away on the anvil with sparks flying, or struggling to get a shoe on a horse's hoof. Down the road was a tree-lined square with a merry-go-round with the owners' wagon nearby. The curtains were always drawn, but sometimes one could see children inside. I thought it must be wonderful to go to sleep in it and wake up in the morning far away.

2

Mama was the fourth of seven children, four brothers and two sisters. She would have loved to study, but this was impossible for a girl at the time [no middle school for girls]. Her brothers had the chance to study [high school] but could not have cared less. She read the *Prague Daily* conscientiously every evening from A to Z.

Very early I assumed responsibility for my younger sisters. With my parents I used to call them "our children." There were two maids, one for household work, the other our nanny. Mama sewed our dresses, mended, darned, and rewove artfully. There were no clothing stores in town. I used to watch her prepare noodles, strudel, dumplings, fats for storage, and wonderful preserved meats. Mama taught us songs and poems in German and Czech, and Grimm and Andersen fairy tales in German only. Weeks before Christmas she began to fold papers in gold and silver for pretty candy containers and colorful chains to adorn the Christmas tree.

There were no automobiles in town, and barefoot, poorly dressed children roamed the streets. I used to play ball in the yard with my mother watching from the kitchen. Once, a group of street kids came to join a game in our yard. After a while they huddled with one of my friends. I heard her say, "But she is not quite Jewish," and the game went on.

There was a frightening fire. The whole of Prague Street seemed to be burning, the flames engulfing house after house in a howling wind. There was the noise of the fire wagons, smoke, eerie flames, people watching from the street. My mother stood on our roof directing the firefighters drenching the rooftops. The fire stopped just short of our house.

3

When I was four years old [1894] my father took me to my maternal grandparents' house for the harvest festival on the seventh day of Sukkoth, one of the few joyous occasions on the Jewish calendar. Grandma Julie [Julia Singer] handed me a gold paper flag with a green Star of David she had made. Grandpa Moritz held my hand as we walked to the nearby synagogue. I was put next to another tot on the front pew and could see Grandpa, president of the community, sitting opposite me near the altar with other dignitaries. Suddenly there was the ominous sound of breaking glass and falling stones. The lights went out. I heard derisive voices shouting from the street and was horrified by the flames I saw through the broken windows. Grandpa reached me in no time. There was panic, everybody trying to get out through the only entrance. I held my eyes closed because I did not want to see the flames. I only heard the howl of the mob and hid my face on Grandpa's shoulder. He comforted me as he carried me home to my parents. My mother cried when she took me in her arms.

I was completely oblivious as to the meaning of this episode. Mama, my mentor, never mentioned religion, though we observed Jewish holidays at home and sometimes at my grandparents' house.

4

At about the same age [four years old] my parents and I drove out to Koloveč (Kollautschen) to visit my paternal grandparents, Samuel Hütter, who was tall and slim, and Theresia Hütter, short, blue-eyed, with blond hair that swept to the floor. My sisters were left at home with the maids. We rode in a yellow Landauer buggy with blue upholstery pulled by a pair of brown horses with black manes [Priam and Palermo, bought at military auction]. We drove through those wonderful Bohemian [dense spruce, fir, and beech] woods. Father said that Little Red Riding Hood's grandmother lived there and that we might meet the wolf, which made me somewhat apprehensive.

Bohemian villages consisted of straw-thatched huts with hissing geese roaming around and mongrels that would snarl and bark. The horses would shy, and Karel the coachman would have to rein them in.

In Koloveč, Grandfather Hütter placed me on a chair to recite poems and sing songs to what he thought would be an admiring audience of country kids listening to a refined city child. My older cousins were crouching on the floor: Anna, Olga, Marie, and Otto Hütter. I was reciting, the children listening, most probably against their will. When my beaming grandfather asked whether they had liked it, they jumped up shouting, "Yes . . ." and rushed out of the room yelling, "but she has red hair!"

Grandfather tore the cap off his head and ran after them to slap them with it. I was stuck on the chair and had to wait until he came back for me. I did not understand yet that "*One je Zlzava*" ["She's ginger," or has red hair] was a stigma for which I would have to make up in other ways to get through life.

When we returned home the horses would show up at the kitchen window begging for sugar. They put their heads inside and refused to leave before being satisfied.

5

That same year [four] I was sent to a kindergarten run by nuns in their convent. I recall feeling overcome with awe at the beautiful chapel with the illuminated virgin adorned with jewels and ribbons and flowers everywhere. My parents must have had second thoughts when I started to present our maids with pictures of saints and exhort them not to work on Sundays. The last straw was my participation in the annual spring procession with the girls all dressed in white carrying lilies, flowers in their hair, a statue of the Madonna at the center of things. The priest marched at the head of the procession holding me by the hand. Most probably it was not known that I was Jewish and the honor bestowed on me because I was the best pupil.

My kindergarten career was terminated not only due to my religious ardor but because I caught and passed on to my little sisters every contagious disease that hit the convent. All three of us had the measles, mumps, and whooping cough to the worst degree. The little ones were spared only my diphtheria at age six. I had played with the two children of the rope maker, who died of the disease. My sisters were taken away to our grandparents. I was unconscious, pursued by a pack of wolves in my dreams.

A serum had just been invented but was not yet available in Klatovy. My father sent one of his employees to Prague, three hours by express train each way, to get it. I recall the injection and the faces of my distraught parents in daylight. I woke up in the dark to the fragrance of fir needles, a Christmas tree hung with candles, and my happy parents. I missed a full term of my first year of school.

6

On evenings when my parents went out, the little girls had to go to bed and I was allowed to stay up longer. The maids in the kitchen used to speak about evil spirits and frightening omens. If they heard dishes clatter in the chest, it meant somebody would die. A bad dream meant disaster. The cry of the *kujíček* bird [folk name for an owl] near a window of a sick child who would not take medicine meant death. They sang the songs of orphaned children and bad stepmothers, which haunted me. There were portents everywhere. Once when I was ill and refused to take my medicine the maids told me that the *kujíček* bird had been flying around the house, which meant he expected my death. I had better take my drops. My parents too were superstitious, and it took many years before I rid myself of all the apprehensions.

....

Childbirth and childhood disease killed many women and children in those days of few vaccines and no antibiotics. After Irma barely survived diphtheria at six, her sister Mela suffered a fever that impaired her mentally and Edna nearly died from croup, a bacterial disease like diphtheria that kills by clogging a child's small lungs and throat. Their youngest sister, Hedi, born premature and frail "with wistful blue eyes," would succumb to influenza and pneumonia at the age of four.

Irma would look back on Klatovy as hopelessly provincial, lacking in cultural venues for music and theater and peopled by uneducated and superstitious characters. I have always liked the way she described the simple entertainment she found there:

7

There was always something to be seen in the streets of the town where nothing seemed to happen. A frequent and welcome sight was a chimney sweep all black with soot, a hat on his head, carrying a ladder and broom. To meet one meant a happy event was just around the corner.

When fairs came to town, booths lined the whole promenade with vendors extolling their wares in loud voices. The children were mainly interested in sweets. Vendors would hold up paper bags with the purchased amount of hard candy, Turkish taffy, dates, and nuts, and throw in another piece "for Adulku or Karlicka," naming any possible sibling. My father would spoil us by buying bangles, earrings, and rings in every color.

A popular figure was Hetepete. She was dressed in rags and did not talk to anybody, and nobody knew where she lived. She went begging from door to door. There were other beggars in town, mostly on street corners and occasionally Gypsies who were said to steal both money and babies.

Another character well known in town was Karliček, either demented or idiotic. He may have been in his twenties and wore a tattered uniform wide open in front over a dirty shirt and a piece of wood representing a sword tied by string around his waist. On his head he wore a military kepi. He danced for a few coins. Occasionally he appeared stark naked. Then he was put in jail for a few days.

There was great excitement when rope walkers came

to town. The rope was slung across the street in our neighborhood, and there was no end of ecstasy and fear.

From time to time a man would show up with a dancing bear and collect pennies in his hat after the show. Some entertainers collected nine kreuzers for a monkey doing tricks. A favorite of the maids was a woman with a parrot who would pick notes forecasting their splendid futures. There were organ grinders who played the first Verdi and Puccini arias I ever heard.

On the occasion of a funeral, a hearse with the coffin was drawn by two horses with black hoods over their heads. It was followed by sharpshooters and a band of musicians playing solemn funeral marches. After the burial they returned from the churchyard playing gay marches and would end up in the inn drinking beer for hours. At the time of army recruiting, young future soldiers from the country with flowers and ribbons on their kepis would roam the streets drunk.

In the spring, tinkers appeared from Slovakia. They were impoverished peasants from the mountain region between Hungary and Poland mending pots and kettles and honing knives. In the fall they would return to their villages with their meager earnings to help their families survive through the harsh winters.

Raithmayer the water carrier was a tall, gaunt, middle-aged man with a wooden yoke across his shoulders holding pails of water to fill bathtubs or scrub floors. The maids had to carry in wood and coal to heat it on the stove in big pots.

Another familiar figure was a tall fellow who lived on handouts from businessmen whom he visited in their stores, telling jokes or funny stories. He knew the birth dates of members of the family and came to offer congratulations on anniversaries or when a child was born, certain of a tip and cigars. At such occasions a band of veterans in their special uniforms, cock feathers on their helmets, would draw up and serenade the happy father.

....

Irma's usually genial father, Johann, was disappointed when his last child, Hedi, was another girl. Legend has it that the band who came to "serenade the happy father" was met with a tub of cold water tossed from the upstairs window. Irma, who already felt responsible for her younger sisters, seems to have assumed the role of family heir.

Irma began life believing that both synagogue and Christmas decorations belonged in her life, that her family had left poverty behind in dusty villages like Koloveč, and that red hair was the only stigma she had to overcome in life. For the rest of her days she would reach toward worldliness and sophistication, and away from the quaint fairy-tale town of Klatovy.

Johann Hütter

Karla Singer Hütter

Getting Better Every Day
1895–1901

——◆◦——————————◦◆——

The narrow "Jewish street" of low stucco houses curves around the edge of the old citadel wall at Strážov (Drosau), the Bohemian village of 1,500 people where Irma's and my ancestors lived for hundreds of years. Here they ran Strážov's shops, sent their children to school with Catholic townsfolk, and attended services at the tiny synagogue. From Strážov's crossroads they traveled overland to ports and fairs trading in silver and iron, forest products and hops from Bohemia, and feathers from distant continents: ostrich, peacock, and ibis plumes for fanciful hats and ornaments.

In time they were laid to rest in the Jewish cemetery two miles out of town where Moritz Singer took his eldest granddaughter in 1895, when she was five years old. Irma felt honored to ride alongside her grandfather in the yellow buggy with blue leather seats on what seemed a long journey to a child, and she nodded off to the regular clop of hooves on packed earth road. They came to a halt near an old stone quadrangle's iron gate and stepped from the tree-lined perimeter into the yard's dappled light. Hundreds of mossy gravestones faintly inscribed in Hebrew lay crookedly about the soft forest floor. Moritz showed Irma how to leave small stones of respect at family graves, among them Moritz's first wife, Marie Lasner, and a sad string of still-born or sickly infants. Irma never found her way back to that ancestral home.

Irma's ancestors had lived in Strážov prior to 1735, when Austrian lawmakers asked Jewish (and Christian) communities to keep records, and possibly as far back as the 1400s. Prohibited to enter many professions, Jews had specialized in useful but risky trade and banking businesses under Catholic landowners and sovereigns who alternately accepted and despised their otherness. Before 1800 they paid taxes for the "privilege" of residency outside town walls or on estates or in cities, and could not migrate freely or own land. But Emperor Franz Josef had swept away the last of such restrictions in 1867, and Strážov's entire Jewish population filtered away for better opportunities. Many set about using knowledge of business, once Jews' only means of support, to trade internationally, open factories, and integrate more deeply into mainstream cultures.

In 1866, thirty-four-year-old Moritz married blond, blue-eyed Julia Kohner Singer, twenty-two, and the family set off around 1869 for Klatovy, seven miles to the north. A new railway built through Klatovy put it on the trade route, displacing Strážov as a crossroads. Moritz expanded from iron trading in Strážov to providing fuel, fodder, food, and agricultural equipment to the huge estates of the Bohemian aristocracy near Klatovy. He bought land at the edge of town and constructed a farm compound where Moritz and Julia raised their six children: Julius, Louise, Siegmund, Karoline (Karla), Josefine, and Emil. Along with Rudolf, Moritz's only living son by his first wife, the family enjoyed a life of middle-class comfort.

Moritz imported goods through German ports. In 1879, Otto

von Bismarck in the German Empire next to Austria slapped a tax on imports to encourage development of domestic industry. Moritz had to pay a financially devastating 100,000 gulden in tax, but he rebuilt his business step by step. Some Strážov Jews left Austria for America, the land of opportunity. Moritz's brothers John (originally Leopold) and Bernard Singer had gone to St. Louis and opened stores, followed by their nephew Rudolf in the early 1870s. After the family business was hit by Bismarck's taxes, Moritz and Julia's children Siegmund and Louise joined them in St. Louis. Irma's paternal aunt, Mary Hütter, left the family's ancestral village of Koloveč to cross the ocean with five friends, and found work as a nanny in New Jersey. Czech girls were said to be good home helpers, and New Yorkers sometimes came to the docks to hire them right off the boat.

Grandma Julie's brother, tall, slim, bronze-bearded Lippmann Kohner, took an alternate route out of Strážov. He went to Vienna, where he grew wealthy on diamond cutting and jewelry selling under the striped awning of the Imperial and Royal Jewelers in the heart of the imperial capital on Kärntner Street at Stephansplatz. Diamonds from his enterprise would reappear as I uncovered links in my research.

Irma remembered her beloved grandparents well:

I

Grandpa was the grand man in the family. He was a poor boy who made good when he was young. Somehow he avoided conscription. A family legend has it that he played deaf and did not budge when a shot went off to test him. He laid the foundation of a prosperous business in great style and saw two brothers off to America before the draft could get them. He accompanied them to Bremerhaven in the 1850s [another record suggests late 1840s], and they settled in St. Louis.

Besides his business he had honorary functions of president of the Jewish community and a position on the Czech town council, a rare honor for a Jew. He provided welfare to the community on a remarkable scale including carloads of coal and wood for the rabbi and Jewish schoolteachers each fall. On Saturdays and holidays the Jewish town pauper was a guest at his table, and poor Jewish boys who came from surrounding villages to study at the Czech high school came for dinner on certain days. Grandma Julie did all the bookkeeping and charitable work for the women's section of the Jewish community, and they both supported the impoverished settlements of Jews in Palestine before Zionism. Grandpa was often out of town in Plzeň, Prague, and Vienna. Every summer he took the cure in Karlsbad Vary spa.

2

Uncle Siegmund, who had migrated to America together with his sister Louise in the early 1880s, came home for the first time in 1898. Uncle Sieg joked that he would return to marry me when I was grown up, and I was very disappointed when two years later he announced his engagement to Stella Shoenfeld, who had a fine voice and money. They went to start an elegant store selling ostrich and egret feathers, artificial flowers, pins, clasps, and hats in Anadarko, Oklahoma Territory, where there was oil and many Indians around. For me it was exciting to hear him talk of that country across the great water and the strange people who lived there. He sang, "Hello my lady, hello my baby," brought me picture books with black children, and told me stories about the Indians. To my dismay I had to show off my accomplishment on the piano by playing Haydn's "Oxen Minuet."

3

A crisis arose in Grandpa Singer's far-flung business enterprises [1898, cause unknown]. Grandpa had diabetes, which the family attributed to financial worries. While trimming his nails, Grandpa Singer injured a toe, which would not heal. Finally, gangrene set in. Professor Pribram, a famous physician at Charles University in Prague, was summoned but could not help. It was the time before insulin.

One day I surprised my mother [Karla] sitting at her desk between the living room windows, crying. My strong mother was under such emotional strain that she must have needed an outlet, for she talked to me as if I were her confidante. To ease her dying father's mind, Mama had persuaded my father to buy Grandpa's property lock, stock, and barrel. The price was set too high, and my father was running into serious difficulties himself. On my mother's desk was a beautiful pin with a large diamond surrounded by rows and circles of smaller diamonds that I'd seen her wear in her hair at wedding celebrations, and a golden collar with diamonds and other precious stones, and rings, and bracelets. She was about to sell them all to tide the family over.

Grandpa was sixty-seven when he died. In Jewish ritual the coffin is of unpainted wood covered by a black shroud with the Mogen David and a few Hebrew words in white, and no flowers. Grandpa's coffin was completely covered by two magnificent wreaths with ribbons. The inscriptions read "To my dear friend and trusted counselor" from Count Czernin and Prince Lobkowicz [famous Bohemian aristocrats].

4

Grandma Julie was still graceful at fifty-four when he died. Her eyes were forget-me-not blue, her blond hair graying. She was very ladylike and had a natural dignity. She was left alone with just the maids in the spacious house. My father took me to Grandma Julie's so she would have company in the evenings for a while. In the mornings one of the maids took me to school. It was still dark, the streets dimly lit by gas lamps, the stores still closed. On their doors I saw rude phrases and crude drawings in chalk: a man dangling from a gallows, under it the name "Hilsner."

I loved my evenings with Grandma. My room was upstairs with the windows facing the courtyard where the rooster crowed each morning. A clock on the wall opposite my bed ticked away. Grandma would take a chair to my bedside and tell stories from past and present. My grandparents were ardent contributors to the small Jewish settlement in Palestine where Russian and Galician [Eastern European] Jews fled bloody persecutions to live and struggle in the land of the Bible. She let me hold lovely books sent in appreciation for their donations, bound in polished Lebanon cedar and exuding the faint smell of flowers pressed in the Holy Land.

She showed me her grandfather's [Salomon Kafka] inscription in a fine hand in one of the first volumes of the Rashi commentaries on the [Hebrew] Bible bound in pig leather, from the early 1800s. It substantiates the story that her mother was brought up on the estate of the Count of Ennis and shared his daughter's [private] education. [Irma implies that the Count fathered both girls].

I was completely unaware of the differences among religions before then, and puzzled when I heard the world "Jew" applied to me in a derisive way, just as I more often felt the stigma of hearing "*Zlzava*" (redhead) as street urchins passed by. Grandma Julie initiated me in Christianity, anti-Semitism, and Palestine [the Holy Land]. All I had experienced was brought into focus by her casual bedside talks. She raised my consciousness of how events reaching into a *dark past* were linked to what was happening then, and affecting me. I became aware of *what it meant to be Jewish* [my italics].

....

How might a devout Jewish grandmother, Julia Singer, explain *what it meant to be Jewish* to eight-year-old Irma? She probably used historical themes of hardship and Jewish resilience. The *dark past* included ancient expulsions, persecution, and segregation in ghettos. Jews had endured by upholding strong communities, educating themselves, and cultivating resilience. Grandma Julie was 24 years old when the good emperor Franz Josef banned religious intolerance, cause of wars, famine, and suffering for Jews, Catholics, Protestants alike. She would have explained that Irma's era was more enlightened than any that came before, while unfounded residual suspicion still tainted some Catholic minds. Grandma Julie's explanation of Irma's otherness would have been like the one given to minority children anywhere.

Austrian Jews practiced their religion and blended into the general population, speaking German and giving up the distinguishing Orthodox customs of long ago. Jews in Russia and Eastern Europe did not have that choice. Unwelcome in general society, they lived separately, lacked access to education, and spoke their own language: Yiddish. Sporadic pogroms, or deadly rampages ignored by police, still took place in those parts of Europe. Some persecuted Jews made their way to tiny religious colonies in the ancient Jewish homeland of Palestine to live in spiritual retreat. Compassion led better-off Jews like Moritz and Julie Singer to donate to Jewish communities in Palestine in addition to their own.

Shadows of the *dark past* lingered in Christian mistrust or prejudice, accounting for the taunts that had puzzled Irma. In 1894, wild rumors of religious desecration had led to the arson at the synagogue that Irma witnessed without comprehension as a tot. The crude gallows image Irma saw on her way to school in 1898 referred to a trial in Eastern Bohemia, in which a poor Jewish vagrant named Hilsner was accused of murdering a Christian woman to obtain blood for ritual matzo-making. Absurd as the charge seemed, it still had the power to inflame Catholic priests and their ardent followers alike.

Grandparents help us connect to the *dark past* from which protective parents are still running. Irma's mother never spoke of religion or prejudice. She embraced assimilation without looking back, and was "enraptured with everything modern," Irma said. But Irma held onto Julie Singer's stories the way I hold onto hers, feeling safely distant from the bad old days.

Irma described her grandparents' house as a place full of her grandparents' spirits. She would create a tribute to the Singer family interior much later in the New World. Irma carries on:

5

We moved to my grandparents' house shortly after Grandpa's passing [1898]. I loved it. It was really a compound enclosing a spacious square yard. In front was the family house with two entrances framed by big oleander trees, one leading to a little store not used in my time. Great-Grandma Anna Lazansky Singer used to play with us there, hiding peppermint drops in her tiny wrinkled fist and making us guess, "*Pinkele, pinkele, welche Hande*" [which hand].

At the left side of the quadrangle was a massive portal through which the ox-drawn carts passed hauling merchandise or harvest. Next were three portals storing sugar in loaves, salt in cones, kerosene in drums. At the back were big stables sheltering forty-six cows, always some calves, two pairs of oxen, and the horses. The herds-man was in charge. He, his wife, and their son had their own household in the adjacent little building. The herds-man and the coachman hated each other. One New Years' night, both drunk, they went at one another with axes, and my parents had to separate them.

The right side consisted of the carriage house for the Landau buggy, carts, and farm implements: plows, harrows, scythes, and sickles, and a doghouse in front for Bulik, the yellow mongrel. The last building at this side was the barn where wheat, barley, and other grains were stored. Inside the courtyard was a tower for pigeons, with a rooster and many hens below.

My delight was the parlor. There were three life-size portraits in gold frames: Grandpa Singer with brown eyes and short dark-blond mustache, looking handsome in his midlife years; Grandma Julie, blond and blue-eyed, wearing a tightly fitting black silk dress and a gold medallion; and Great-Grandma Anna Kafka Kohner, blond with violet eyes. The furniture was exqui-site Biedermeier, including glass-fronted cabinets lined with Brussels lace with porcelain figurines, antiques in silver and gold, and Bohemian crystal in blue and red with family monograms. Sofa and chairs were grace-fully upholstered in emerald-green wool and silk. Three silver chandeliers hung in the parlor, dining room, and master bedroom.

6

1898 marks a milestone in my life. It seems as if I were stepping out of the semi-darkness of a dreamland into the clear light of consciousness. The schoolroom [annex to the synagogue] was drab. Classes were taught in German with one hour in Czech. Only the few Jewish families had remained speaking German [preferring the more universal and refined language over the local Czech in school; Czechs had fought hard in Austria's parliament to win the right to teach in Czech instead of the imperial language, German]. We had a strong Czech accent, which I later tried desperately to get rid of. The conversational language at that time was "*Küchel Böhmisch*," the language of the common people. I suspect we children spoke Czech amongst ourselves.

Suddenly school became important. I became a voracious reader, reading anything I could lay my hands on. For me the world began to open up. There were the languages with their different grammars—German, Czech, and later Latin—and math problems like squaring and cubing that I found to be exciting, plus the never-ending delight of Greek mythology. There were Rabbi Wolf's weekly classes in religion with Hebrew songs, benedictions, and biblical sayings that came strictly from the Hebrew Bible [Old Testament]. No mention was ever made of Christ, Mary, or the Apostles.

I loved to go to school and come home to read and read, much to the disapproval of Grandma Julie, who thought a girl should help in the kitchen or do other useful work, like mending, darning, knitting socks or stockings, crocheting, or embroidering. Mama supported me in my reading. She worried about my higher education. There was no German high school in town, and girls were not accepted in the Czech one.

At the age of nine I read my first book from the library, *Der Kleine Dauphin (The Little Crown Prince),* about the flight of Louis XVI and Marie Antoinette with their two children and their return to Paris. It was the first time I had heard of the French Revolution, and I was horrified. My country, Austria, had not known war for many decades. I learned in school that all previous wars had been instigated by our enemies. I was thankful for living in an enlightened era a century later, when such terrible things were impossible. I took comfort in the thought that in my own lifetime the world was getting better every day.

Irma as Titania, Queen of Fairies, 1906

Away to the City

České Budějovice, 1901–1910

—◆•————————•◆—

I rma was eleven years old in the summer of 1901 when the
Hütter family boarded the steam train at Klatovy station and
chugged sixty-five miles westward to Southern Bohemia's regional
hub of České Budějovice (Chesky Bood yo vitza, or Budweis in
German). Opportunity and education beckoned. All over the
Austrian Empire, people were leaving rural villages for modern
urban possibilities. Industry was hauling people out of poverty,
urban factories were hiring, and deadly diseases like diphtheria
were being conquered by medical breakthroughs. Steamships and
train networks were making leisure travel more affordable.

European parliaments were considering opening up higher
education to girls and extending voting rights to men of all ranks.
Most significantly, Klatovy lacked a middle school for girls, such
that Irma's mother Karla's education had ended at age eleven. She
was not going to let her gifted daughter suffer the same constraint.
At her instigation, the Hütters leased their Klatovy land for a
chemical factory, packed up their daughters Irma (11), Mela (9),
Edna (8), and the delicate Hedi (4), and joined the migration.

Karla Hütter's forcefulness marches straight out of Irma's text. Karla: the woman who climbed atop the roof to direct firefighters when Klatovy was burning, who sold her diamonds to help buy her father's business when he was ailing, who devoured newspapers when women didn't, and the woman Irma called strong-willed, enterprising, ambitious, modern, her mentor.

České Budějovice's population of forty-five thousand was four times Klatovy's eleven thousand. The central square's jigsaw storefronts and cobblestone yard scaled larger than Klatovy's, the churches and ornately modern synagogue rose grander, and the middle school for girls was well-established. Wide avenues bustled with horse-drawn wagons from the Budweiser Bier brewery, the sawmill, and the graphite pencil, porcelain, and metal factories. Anheuser-Busch aspired to the style of Budweis, the city's German name, when it named its American beer.

The Hütters chose Budějovice because three of Karla's siblings were already there. Five or ten years earlier, Karla's sister Josefine left a failed romance in Klatovy and married wealthy merchant Karl Sinek there. Karla's brother Julius and his wife, Berta, left Vienna, where Julius had worked for his uncle Lippmann Kohner's diamond business. He took a job in Budějovice representing insurance giant Assicurazioni Generali. Karla's youngest brother, Emil, finished his legal education and joined them there before he married and later moved to Brno (Brünn), Moravia. Grandma Julie went to live with Julius until the Hütters settled in. Karla's aunt Eva (Emma) Singer Winternitz had her own large house nearby. The Hütter girls would get to know their aunts, uncles, and cousins: Mizzi and Vali Sinek, and Paul and Ernst Singer.

Budějovice was a *Deutsche Sprachinsel* (a German linguistic island), *surrounded by a Slavonic sea* in the phrase of the time. German linguistic islands dated back to the thirteenth century when Germanic tribes were invited to repopulate the landscape after plagues and wars. German-speaking Austrians had held onto power and entitlement in those urban outposts, but by 1901 almost half the city's people were Czechs who had migrated in from the surrounding countryside. The established *German Liberals* were losing their voting majority to newly enfranchised ethnic Czechs. The German island was being flooded by the Slavonic sea.

"German" meant a language and a set of cultural values, not a country. The Hapsburg family was *as German as* the Prussians, Bavarians, and Saxons in the German Empire next door. Common *German* aspirational values included principled self-discipline, respect for education, and appreciation for high arts like classical music and literature—all extolled as *German* in a body of writing. Irma and her family were German in their acceptance of those mainstream values.

German was the official language of the Austrian Empire, spoken by sixty million people in the world compared to five million for Czech. Germans disparaged Czech as a "peasant dialect," and educated Jews leaned the same way. Living side by side in pluralistic rather than integrated communities, the German and Czech Austrians tended to favor their own languages and customs even when they were fully bilingual. České Budějovice's Hardtmuth pencil factory employed only German Austrians; the Budweiser Bier brewery employed only Czech Austrians. Each had their own social clubs. Middle-class Jews like Irma's family belonged to the German group and frequented the stately red brick clubhouse, Deutsches Haus (German House).

Ethnically Czech Bohemians and Moravians had a glorious past of their own and bridled under German assumptions of cultural superiority. They sought more autonomy in a time when calling for independence would have been treated as seditious. Some Austrian Germans, in backlash against a slow loss of entitlement, bolstered their sense of cultural superiority with newfound "racial" superiority over all others. Some imagined political unity with fellow ethnic Germans concentrated in the German Empire.

Scholar Jeremy King used Irma's teen home to illustrate how rising ethnic nationalism was fraying old social contracts in his book *Budweisers into Czechs and Germans*. He wrote of the period when Budějovice mayor Josef Taschek, father of Irma's friend Klara, led the old *German Liberal* party in trying to hold the city together as one people. Taschek, a Czech, relied on the Jewish lawyer Israel Kohn as a partner in quashing efforts by racialist *German Nationals* to reject Jews, or to oust them from German clubs, calling their intolerance "un-German."

German Austrians in Vienna feared that their power would be diluted by minorities. Emperor Franz Josef struggled for an inclusive unity. He had refused to instate Karl Lueger as elected mayor of Vienna because Lueger's winning coalition catered to anti-Semitic German factions. After Lueger won a second round in 1897, the emperor had to relent and instate him.

In the same time frame, turn-of-the-century Austria, a Jewish nationalist movement called Zionism was born in Vienna around ideas of Jewish solidarity. Although Irma was unaware that a much-whispered-about bachelor named Jakob Ehrlich was involved, she did know that he worked in the law office of Israel Kohn, Mayor Taschek's lawyer, and that he climbed mountains with ropes and ice picks.

The Hütters were not averse to a Czech pride movement, nor did they belong to it naturally. After all, it was Catholic Czechs who attacked the synagogue, roved the streets barefoot and unschooled, arrived as maids never having seen a tooth-brush, and went after each other with axes like the herdsman and coachman back in Klatovy. Irma's family admired Tomáš Masaryk, Bohemia's parliamentary representative who had once defended the poor Jewish vagrant Hilsner against blood libel charges and was advocating for educational opportunity and voting rights for women in Vienna. Johann Hütter had his first chance to vote in 1907 when the franchise opened to men regardless of income. The busy family probably did not talk about politics at home.

All of this was offstage, not important to Irma, who was just beginning to notice social divisions as she found her place in the world. She was not burdened by fear of prejudice. Red or golden hair, once stigmatized, had come roaring into fashion "just in time," she said. Her place was onstage at Deutsches Haus, as we see in the 1906 photograph of Irma at fifteen or sixteen. She is Shakespeare's fairy queen Titania in a feminine sweep of voile, her oval face framed by a massive mane of Titian ringlets: proud, self-possessed, charismatic. She was learning to captivate an audience, hold them in her thrall, and win their admiration. At sixteen she was an Austrian girl of Bohemia, Jewish, clever, classically beautiful.

Like many Europeans she would barely have noticed when Austria annexed Bosnia and Herzegovina in 1908, and Slavic nationalistic Czechs rioted in the streets against German supremacism. Resentment against the annexation would lead to cataclysmic events in young Irma's life.

When the Hütters moved to Budějovice in 1911, life was difficult at first. Irma's parents were uprooted. Klatovy had a factory for men's shirts, and Irma's enterprising mother succeeded in finding a wealthy man interested in investing in a Budějovice branch. It failed. They opened an outlet for nails and screws of the Kopperl and Blasskopf factories, but it was not profitable. At last Irma's parents specialized in kitchenware of the finest quality. The store was open Saturdays and Sundays until noon. Her strong-willed, ambitious mother became her father's full-fledged business partner. Home life changed drastically; it was no joy to come home from school because only the maids were there. A family tragedy struck.

When Irma wrote her memories of this time, her Czech homeland was inaccessible. Soviet forces had invaded Czechoslovakia in 1968, crushing the Czech longing for independence. This must have added to her feelings of tenderness for a lost past. A grandchild on her knee always brought one lilting song to Irma's lips: "*Muss I' denn, muss I' denn, zum Städtele hinaus,*"—"Away to the City"—a song of nostalgia for country hearth and home, a song about Klatovy for Irma. I felt the same way about leaving rural Massachusetts at age eleven for an uncertain future in a different regional city, St. Louis, Missouri.

She wrote:

I

We moved to Budějovice in the summer. The fall was chilly and rainy. Hedi caught the flu, which turned into pneumonia. I recall the corner of the room where I offered God my most cherished possessions for Hedi's life all night long. In the adjoining room my parents kept vigil. The next day was a beautiful Friday. The sun was shining. Someone came to ask for my relief from school. As we passed a church on the way home from school, a bell rang: three o'clock. Hedi had died.

I was not admitted to the boys' academic high school that was run by Premonstratensian monks [apparently Karla had the gumption to try to get her in] and was enrolled in the only girls' middle school in a large building. I was a newcomer among ninety-two girls, seated on the last bench in an enormous room. All were Catholic with the exception of eight Jewish girls. Most of the others had gone through grade school together. I felt uneasy and left out when I had to stand idly by while the girls around me made the sign of the cross and said their prayers loudly.

A class of ninety-two pupils with different backgrounds must have been a difficult assignment for a teacher.

School hours were 8–12 and 2–4. My parents came home for lunch because shops were closed midday, and I would tell stories. "*Irmicko, povidah*," my father used to say: "Irma, tell," and he would laugh tears about the funny stories I had to tell. It shows he liked to speak Czech.

Next to me sat a kid completely oblivious of what was going on. Her father was a worker at the Hardtmuth pencil factory. She copied from me freely, and whenever I prompted her, she stuffed my pencil holder with [free] pencils.

Our teacher was a pedantic, uninspiring spinster [women gave up teaching at marriage] named Katarina Kunz. Her widowed mother, Katarina Senior, toothless with an ever-mobile chin, taught us women's handicrafts like knitting, crocheting, mending, darning, and embroidering. She would exhort us, "A decent young girl does not leave the house without gloves."

We had to memorize poems, which most of the kids hated or could not remember. Miss Kunz asked for a volunteer to recite. I was not even aware that my arm shot up in the last bench. No one else volunteered. I was called to the platform and recited Uhland's "*Des Sängers Fluch*," ("The Minstrel's Curse"), a highly dramatic piece. I was amazed to hear my voice. In the unruly class one could have heard a needle drop.

On the next occasion the whole class shouted my name: "Hütter! Hütter!" My report at the end of the term was "outstanding" without any effort on my part. From then on, I was a kind of star, singled out for special occasions. Only my performance in women's handiwork was imperfect because I was not interested in knitting socks.

It had not taken long to make friends and become accepted. My standing in school was of great help, but

I was bored from the point of view of learning during the three years of middle school. Fortunately there were a few sources of interest. Mama took care of it. There was Madame Pescke, a highly efficient French teacher who spoke Swiss-French and let us speak with our German-Czech accents; and Mrs. Schick, the uninspiring piano teacher. One or two years later there was English with Miss Smith, a Scot. On Wednesday afternoons there were gymnastic lessons with Mr. Richter at *Deutsches Haus*, which were great fun.

2

I do not remember having been at the homes of my classmates, with the exceptions of the Christmas parties at the home of Klara Taschek, whose father was the mayor, and in the *keller* (cellar) of the Budweiser Bier Brewery, where we were invited by the chief brewer, Mr. Peter, father of Betty Peter.

Mayor Taschek was highly regarded as a *German Liberal* party politician. Klara was the youngest of four daughters, a pampered child. At Christmas her parents gave her a big party, and it was a special distinction to be selected among her schoolmates. We were treated to a sumptuous banquet with no end of delicacies. It speaks to the fair-mindedness of the mayor and his family that Jewish children were invited.

We were newcomers and my parents busy, and I think there was little socializing in the town. People moved mostly in their family circles, which I found boring. My parents' steady company on Sundays and holidays were Uncle Julius and Aunt Berta and their two little boys with whom, weather permitting, we would hike along the unpaved roads into the country past meadows of poppies, daisies, buttercups, clover, cornflowers, and for-get-me-nots in wet places. Our destination was an inn with a shady garden, picnic tables, and good rustic food to serve: fresh bread and butter, beer or coffee, lemon soda for the kids.

Budějovice lies in a wide river valley, not a mountain in sight, and my dreams were always of mountains. I had never seen one. I knew from friends that there was an elite circle of men who had studied in Vienna and spent their weekends taking the late train on Fridays the three hours to Adolfstal in the Bohemian woods to climb the one-thousand-meter Schöniger. Regulars were Dr. Ehrlich and Dr. Benisch of Dr. Kohn's law office, the physician Dr. Reiter, and others of the professional smart set [the title "Dr." indicates a university degree]. I was stuck with those hikes with kith and kin.

3

In my youth there was an awakening of Czech national fervor and resistance against German supremacy in Austria. In Vienna one did not hear the music of Czech composers Josef Suk, Leoš Janáček, Antonín Dvořák, and Vítězslav Novák, but it was played in Prague. Dvořák and Bedřich Smetana made the Czech national dances world-renowned. There was a generation of authors eager to purify the commonly spoken Czech language and an awakening of literature from Jaroslav Vrchlický, Karel Čapek, and Friedrich Hayek. The politicians Tomáš Garrigue Masaryk, Václav Klofáč, and Karel Kramář taught at the University of Prague and fought in parliament for Bohemia's rights.

There was music, singing, dancing all over the country. A poor peasant might have a fiddle. When the windows were open the maids were singing while working. One could hear someone from across the street chime in, harmonizing with the first voice. Young people loved to dance polka, mazurka, and *šlapák*. The girls wore costumes on festive occasions: short red skirts, white blouses, black velvet corsets, and on the head, the "little pigeon," an ornament of white ribbons. The men wore knee pants and short jackets.

When I was fourteen I was sent to Uncle Simon and Aunt Katy Hütter in Koloveč during my summer vacation. I was thin and growing fast, and Mama said I needed country air. Koloveč [30 miles to the south of Budějovice] was a village without charm. Uncle Simon's house and store were at the corner of the unpaved main street near a pond with innumerable geese. But at a distance of half an hour were those wonderful dark woods of pine and fir with thick layers of moss and lichen sprinkled with the glowing red of wild strawberries and an inexhaustible abundance of mushrooms. Those woods forming the border between Bohemia and Bavaria were of awe-inspiring beauty, dense and dark with the light flickering through the majestic trees. We never met anyone. The forests belonged to the animals, birds, bees, and insects. I was in the company of my cousins Anna, Olga, Marie, Otto, and sometimes Emil, who was older and studying mathematics in Prague.

The Bohemian Forest had famous spas [resort towns]. Aficionados swore they found the cure for all kinds of afflictions in the mineral waters. Mariánské Lázně (Marienbad) was a favorite of Aunt Josefine Singer Sinek. She invited me to accompany her when I was fourteen. My aunt was jolly and outgoing and always had company. One day we heard English at the next table. Without hesitation my aunt called out: "I have a brother in America." One of the men at the other table answered in German, and it was established in no time that he was my uncle Rudolf's business partner in St. Louis. People went to Mariánské Lázně to lose weight. It was a delightful place with elegant hotels surrounded by wonderful forests. Visitors came from all over the world to take the mineral waters. King Edward VII of England and his entourage of beautiful women were present. Music was everywhere. There my cousin, young and handsome physician Dr. Paul Singer, met and married his baroness. After two weeks I had to return because I had accepted my first job: to coach a girl for an exam. I bought Shakespeare's works in German with my first self-earned money.

The people of northwest Bohemia's spa region and southwest Bohemia's forests were German, haters of the Czechs, and when time became ripe, ardent Nazis. [These are the border regions later claimed by Hitler as German Sudetenland].

My parents had never traveled before. Now, in the following years while I was still at home, Mama, my sisters, and I spent one summer month in the Alps, starting in Windischgarsten, Upper Austria. It was a lovely resort in the Bohemian woods spreading across the border into Bavaria to the foot of the Arber, the highest mountain in the range, elevation 1,400 meters. The air was saturated with fragrance. One day we met a friend of Mama's youth who volunteered to take me up the Arber. Nothing more wonderful could have happened to me. We passed the dark waters of Arber Lake, over huge boulders on a poorly marked trail. I had my first unforgettable view from the mountain.

This was a perfect vacation, and I had only one sad memory. A lady in our hotel was always dressed in black in the midst of a beautiful summer. Her husband had been killed in the notorious pogrom of Kishinev in Poland [49 Jewish residents killed, 500 injured, 1,500 homes attacked by a mob led by Catholic priests in 1903. This reinforced the Austrian Jewish view that Eastern Europe was hostile and uncivilized].

Bohemia was rich in natural resources. There was uranium in Jáchymov. The Sudetenland was rich in coal mines. In the poverty-stricken Krkonoše, women in convents made exquisite embroidery. My mother started collecting a dowry when I was twelve years old. I had twelve dozen linen bed sets and twelve sets of embroidered tablecloths with napkins.

Karlovy Vary (Karlsbad) was famous both for its spas and its centuries-old manufacture of porcelain. The Bohemian woods had its famous etched crystal glassware in white, blue, and red. Jablonec exported tasteful costume jewelry. Budějovice had a factory for candy, Fuerth; the great Hardtmuth pencil factory; and the world-famous brewery, Budweiser Bier. Equally famous were the beers of Plzeň and Smíchov. Saaz provided hops for the breweries. In Chotěboř, hundreds of workers were busy making wigs of Chinese hair.

4

Deutsches Haus was the center of the upper-class German society in Budějovice, along with Kaffee Haus on the town square. Ladies of leisure, not my mother, would meet there afternoons to play cards, or just gossip. Deutsches Haus was beautifully located at the Malše (Maltsche) shortly before its confluence with the Vltava

River (Moldau). It had a garden with old shade trees, benches, and a field where we had our gymnastics during the warm season.

At fifteen I was thin, pale, an insatiable reader. I was completely naive and thought of myself as a kind of misfit with my golden hair. At sixteen a metamorphosis occurred. I grew, people asked what kind of secret creams I used for my complexion—there was no makeup at the time, yet my skin was immaculately white and always rosy. My professor of literature began to point out some of my features: profile Greek, hair Nordic. My schoolmates nicknamed me "Isolde."

I was invited to perform the leading part at one of the seasonal balls of the Jewish community on the stage of Deutsches Haus. I was known for my recitals, and my role was a world traveler. I had visited the most distant and exotic parts of the world and rattled off the most unpronounceable names. It was a great success.

In those faraway days there was a great distance between teacher and pupil. I never talked privately to any of them. Once during intermission I was standing alone near a window. Professor Glass passed by and said casually, "*Mademoiselle, vous serez une grande amoureuse*" ("You will be a woman of passion"). Usually German was used in class. I was quite naive and wondered why he said it and what he meant.

Tanzstunde (dance hour) was a great event for teenagers in the fall–winter season. The lessons were given Saturday evenings in the ballroom of Deutsches Haus. Our partners were boys of about the same age or a couple of years older, mostly students of the academic high school or trade school. Each girl was accompanied by a chaperone. In two separate rows girls and boys practiced the steps. Afterwards the boys chose their partners for the dance. We learned polka, mazurka, Austrian ländler, waltz, polonaise, quadrille, and a formal gallop with which the ball ended.

It was rather with trepidation that I saw the first evening approaching. Since leaving Klatovy I had not known a single boy. What kind of talk would they be interested in? Most of them were students in the academic high school—so should I talk of Goethe and Schiller? I did just that, I think. My fears dissipated and I became popular. The couples tried their dances to the music of the loveliest operettas of Straus, Lehár, Millöcker, and Suppe. Lehár's *Die Lustige Witwe* (*The Merry Widow*) was the new rage of the day. Also *Ein Walzertraum* [*A Waltz Dream* by Oscar Straus], with its softly lilting rhythms. Waltz was the favorite. At the final ball of *Tanzstunde* as on evening walks, Rudolf Kohn was my partner.

In Budějovice six to seven p.m. was the hour for a constitutional along the town square. Teenagers strolled on one side, older couples on another, and peasant girls with their soldier boyfriends on a third. Girls walked arm in arm. Since *Tanzstunde,* young men would appear and ask for permission to join at the side of the girl he adored. My friend Anny Freund and I were always flanked on both sides. In summer the walks would be along the Krumlauer Allee with its spectacular old linden trees, along the river to the rapids near the Geller sawmill, where floats of trees from the Bohemian woods tumbled down the rapids with rowers standing on top shouting commands.

5

In 1904 a committee of ladies of the higher German bourgeoisie founded a German girls' academic high school [also reported in England in the 1904 issue of *Womanhood* magazine], starting with two classes as an experiment. It was a stroke of fortune for me, though at a loss of at least two years. The school started with a first- and third-year class [of four]. There were nine Jewish and nine Catholic girls, and one Protestant [20 percent carried on from middle school, including all of the Jewish girls].

The school was on a quiet side street in a drab old civic building. The classes were in long rooms with two rows of old-fashioned benches, two girls to each bench, with a narrow corridor and no room to go outdoors. A joke likened it to a poor schoolhouse in America. We had, however, many good teachers and most of the girls were eager to learn. Little Magda Klinger commuted daily from Český Krumlov (Krumau) —a lengthy train ride [now a two-hour drive]. There were of course those who filled in time before getting married to whomever was presented to them as a suitable match.

In hindsight it strikes me that the Catholic girls sat together at one side. Marie von Kohoutek, a latecomer during the last two years, a Protestant, the tallest and oldest, sat alone on the last form behind the Jewish girls. Marie was highly gifted and became my best friend. Her father had been a general; with his changing garrisons she had seen much of the Austrian Empire, while most other girls were utterly provincial. During the summer her mother rented a house at Adolfstal [nearest mountain resort, eastern edge of the Bohemian woods] and invited me.

I do not think that anti-Semitism was responsible for the seating order at this time. It may have been social grounds. Budějovice had a big garrison and attracted the widows of high-ranking officers like the von Kohouteks. They kept to themselves. [Social and political] rifts ran through families. Most of the upper-class Germans were *German Nationals.* They did not mix [but they used Deutsches Haus for their meetings]. Mariechen Stegman was a tomboy with pink cheeks. Her father owned a metal factory, one of the few *German Liberals* of the bourgeoisie in town. He was a jovial man who mixed with us Jewish girls. Maus Westen, Mariechen's cousin, kept strictly aloof.

Next to me sat Erna Kohn, daughter of the lawyer Dr. Israel Kohn. We had written exams in class occasionally and Erna copied directly from me, which gave her away. I had to be punished for not having stopped her. The next report my mark for English was *lobenswert* (laudable), the only time I did not have a straight *verzüglich* (outstanding).

6

Our teachers were Premonstratensian priests of the Hohenfurt order who had previously taught exclusively at the boys' high school. We had professors for French and English, and later also science, literature, history, and geography. The highly efficient—though often drunk—Professor Krogner taught literature. Considering Professor Krogner's political views and his belief in the German nation's superiority, it can be assumed that in due time he became an ardent National Socialist [successor to the *German National* party]. The French he characterized as decadent, profligate, immoral, not to be trusted, unscrupulous. Italians were "*Katzelmacher*," meaning unreliable, not to be taken seriously. England was "Perfidious Albion," her motto: *divide et impera* (divide and conquer), power hungry. Russia was a giant with clay feet. America was a new land of opportunities. Her upper crust of multimillionaires, the Rockefellers, Astors, Vanderbilts, and Mellons, were greedy exploiters and robber barons. The population was made up of the remnants of Indian tribes, Negroes, the scum and outcasts of Europe. South America was a bunch of ridiculous operetta republics.

Germany alone was supreme [according to Krogner]. Her people [including Austrian Germans] were the master race. "*Deutschland, Deutschland über alles, über alles in der Welt*": Germany is supreme. "*Am deutschen Wesen soll die Welt genesen*": The German way of life will heal the world. "*Deutschland, das Land der Dichter und Denker*": Germany, the land of the poets and philosophers. Apart from his Germanophilia, Professor Krogner was an excellent teacher, acquainting us with Goethe, Schiller, Heine, and great German art, and we followed him readily, young as we were.

One of the best teachers was Professor Glass [the one who had mused about her passionate nature. Note her hint below that he may have been gay]. It was rumored he had been demoted from Vienna for some unknown reason. He was arrogant, sarcastic, and apparently felt superior to his provincial environment. He did not mix socially, seems to have been a bachelor. One saw him only in company with another French professor, a newcomer in town. He spoke elegant French, ridiculed our pronunciation, and gave lots of homework. Magda Klinger was of Český Krumlov, a petite little girl. Once she was reprimanded by Professor Glass for something:

"*Magda, sind Sie ein deutsches Mädchen?*" ("Are you a (well behaved) German girl?")

She quipped back, "*Ich bin kein deutsches Mädchen.*" ("I'm not a German girl.")

He, amused, "*Was sind Sie dann?*" ("What are you then?") She, proudly: "*Eine Jüdin.*" ("I am a Jewess.")

[She refused to equate good behavior and *German* identity.] There was a strong Zionist group in Český Krumlov. It was the first time I heard of Zionism [the Jewish pride movement].

During the last two years Dr. Karl Thieber, new in town, was our religion teacher. His classes were so interesting that even Marie von Kohoutek, a Protestant, attended. He taught comparative religions and was a bachelor. So was Dr. Haim, the surgeon, and Dr. Jakob Ehrlich, a concipient or young lawyer who must practice with an established law firm before striking out on his own. He was employed at the prestigious office of Dr. Israel Kohn. The three had studied in Vienna. They were highly acclaimed in society, particularly Dr. Ehrlich, who was strikingly handsome. At parties that I attended when I was seventeen, they were seen together and did not dance. Once after a performance on the stage at Deutsches Haus at a Hanukkah party, he asked me for a dance.

We were brought up far from a cultural center without any idea of what was happening in the world. At my time a young girl was not to read a newspaper lest she could be spoiled by learning about things she was supposed not to know. Only in the course of time by outside influences and reading did I begin to question and to think independently. With all our limitations, we were happy. These were carefree and innocent days.

Irma and Erwin in Trieste, 1914

The Accidental Zionist
in Prague
1910–1914

✦————✦

Nineteen-year-old Irma Hütter leaned lightly into the iron fretwork fence over the Vltava River, letting her eyes waltz from spire to enchanting spire—just like the young woman in an etching she treasured from that time. Three golden spindles topped Strahov Monastery, built, plundered, and restored over eight centuries. A congregation of red rooftops surrounded the graceful Baroque cupola of St. Nicholas Church. Four black-bronze spears guarded the Gothic west tower of Charles Bridge as Prague Castle jutted massively upward from behind. In Prague, a city that had been building spires for a thousand years, Irma had reached her own pinnacle.

As a student at Charles University, symbol of learning and enlightenment since 1347, Irma felt like a Titian-haired swan out of Koloveč's ugly duckling pond. Her indulgent father and willful mother had put her through high school as though she were a son and heir, just as Austria's universities opened to women in the early 1900s. Of the 1 percent of Austrian youths who reached university in those years, just 4 percent were women. In other words, the ratio of elite one-percenter men to a vanguard of exceptional women on campus was 25:1 (or 2500:1 among college-age youths in Austria). Public opinion assumed that attractive women would not want to be scholars and that educated women might not find marriage partners. Irma found crowds of young gallants vying to carry her books, just for the pleasure of her company.

Irma arrived in Prague with stacks of voluminous bloomers, petticoats and pintucks, and weighty wool ankle-length skirts that kicked out satisfyingly on a brisk walk. Also in her traveling chest was a navy-blue woolen knit sack covering neck to knees for swimming in the Vltava, and a ball gown—which I know because she asked during my skuzzy jeans-and-boots college years: "Have you been to any balls lately?"

Shortly after arrival, a registrar's question stumped her for a second: at a time when student meals came from dining halls, would she dine as an Orthodox or Zionist Jew? She was not Orthodox: ultra-religious, restrictive, and separate, like the Jewish students from Eastern Europe. She was not Zionist: political and socially rebellious, like Magda Klinger. Between the two, Zionists were at least modern, and so, in an instant, Zionism pried its way unbidden into her life.

Irma enrolled in the mainstream German-speaking college at Charles University for a classical education in humanities. Others studied in the practical streams of law, medicine, or theology, or at the Czech-speaking affiliate where Bohemian and Moravian ethnic Czechs could assert the validity of their native tongue. For Irma, German was the language of the highly educated, preferable for its vast body of scholarship and literary history. She took classes in history, philosophy, art, and languages as she pondered her major. French seemed a natural choice, but she was also intrigued by the great books of England. In her English literature class, she noticed a pale student with dark hair who slumped like a bug in the first row. His name was Franz Kafka, a distant relative (Irma's maternal great-grandmother was born a Kafka) on his way to defining a uniquely Czech body of literature. Opposite that classroom, a large crowd of students lined the halls waiting for a wild-haired physics professor by the name of Albert Einstein. Charles University had offered him his first full professorship, and there, in 1911, Einstein made the calculations that led to his theory of general relativity.

Irma set about shaping the cosmopolitan lady she aspired to be. She dropped Czech sibilance from her German, shed the last vestige of a guttural German R for a proper rolling French one, and worked on her limited English. Her friends were surprised when she decided to major in English, which was far less popular than French. Perhaps her choice had something to do with her English professor. Dr. Erwin Kolmar had warm brown eyes, a puckish mustache twirled into points, elfin ears, and a quick, athletic way of moving. He was remarkably young for a professor, just four years her senior; Jewish; Bohemian Austrian; and an avid mountaineer. Like many university men, Dr. Kolmar had carried on with officer training beyond his obligatory military service. Officer status protected Jewish men from squalor in the ranks and demonstrated patriotism.

Dr. Kolmar's specialty was philology, especially the evolution of Old English (Saxon) to Middle English (the language of Chaucer). For her thesis he helped Irma to choose a narrative poem by Samuel Butler called "Hudibras," a satirical seventeeth-century polemic against militance, hypocrisy, and religious intolerance written after the English Civil War between Catholics and Protestants. Considerable time with the brilliant professor would have been required to grasp it:

> For his Religion, it was fit
> To match his learning and his wit;
> 'Twas Presbyterian true blue;
> For he was of that stubborn crew

Of errant saints, whom all men grant
To be the true Church Militant;
Such as do build their faith upon
The holy text of pike and gun;
Decide all controversies by
Infallible artillery;
And prove their doctrine orthodox
By apostolic blows and knocks;
Call fire and sword and desolation,
A godly thorough reformation,
Which always must be carried on,
And still be doing, never done;
As if religion were intended
For nothing else but to be mended.

As the thesis developed, so did feelings between professor and student. Dr. Kolmar invited Irma to row on the Vltava, pulling upriver under the arched stone bridges to drift lazily back downstream. Just before the waters schussed through the weir at Charles Bridge like tresses through a comb, he rowed upriver again. On such a day, with the river near flood stage, he miscalculated; the boat capsized and threw them into the river.

Irma loved sweeping up and down rivers in her stately breaststroke. She should have bobbed to the surface as Erwin did, but the pounding waterfall kept her under until she floated up, ghostly and unconscious. Erwin tried desperately to breathe life back in; a bystander tied her hair out of the way with a red bandana. Irma's eyes opened to Erwin, and love was lit. Next, Irma noticed the red bandana, a violation of our redheads' color code, and snatched it away. They were quarantined for fear of cholera in the floodwaters, and from then on, became partners in romance.

....

Prague's venerable town squares, clubs, coffee houses, and salons seethed with intellectual ferment. Earnest students debated classical and traditional concepts amidst a flurry of modernist ideas, many of them influenced by the psychological insights of Sigmund Freud. In Vienna, author Arthur Schnitzler was revealing his characters' inner conflicts in a style later called stream of consciousness. Austrian composer Arnold Schoenberg was disrupting the old rules of harmony with atonal music. In France, painters Pablo Picasso and Henri Matisse were rejecting traditional perspective, while in Berlin, Paul Klee and Wassily Kandinsky were inventing abstraction. Philosophers and literary figures like existentialist Martin Buber, writer Max Brod, and his friend Franz Kafka gathered at the home salon of Berta Fanta, who also hosted musical evenings in which Albert Einstein played his violin.

Exhilarated by life among the intelligentsia, Irma learned to hold her own in any conversation. While she was mainly interested in art and literature, others explored national and ethnic identity. Czech students joined Sokol (Falcon), a fitness club associated with ethnic pride, and developed defining ideas of a Czech national character and liberation from German influence. They felt that Czechs deserved greater autonomy in proportion to the region's contribution to the empire. Eighty percent of Austria's industrial capacity lay in Czech and Slovak territory. Austrian culture was invigorated by Czech-born figures like Gustav Mahler from Bohemia and Sigmund Freud from Moravia. Some dreamed of full independence as a nation, though to demand statehood would have been traitorous.

German clubs discussed whether self-discipline, structured thinking, and artistic appreciation were exceptional traits in ethnic Germans, and whether mixing with non-Germans polluted their stock. Some ultra-German student clubs sang nationalistic songs, exercised in military formation, and brawled with Czechs and Jews when drunk.

The university's foreign students included many Russian Jews because of limits on Jewish education in Russia. Their numbers helped swell Jewish student ratios, especially in medicine (about 40 percent Jewish) and law (about 25 percent). Some Austrian Germans complained that Jews, just 4 or 5 percent of the empire, were consuming more than their share of higher education and should be allotted their seats by quota. Irma had laughed off her tipsy high school literature professor's romance with German supremacism, but the same notions were surprisingly resilient at university.

In an enlarged photo from 1910 of the Bar Kochba club, the Association of Jewish Academics in Prague, is a recognizable face with elfin ears and a curlicue moustache: Dr. Erwin Kolmar, twenty-four, professor of philology. Jewish academics gathered at Bar Kochba to define modern Jewishness just as Czech thinkers were raising a Czech national consciousness and Germans were honing theirs. Bar Kochba members weighed the ideas of Zionism, a nascent movement being defined in clubs like theirs at universities across Europe. *Cultural Zionism* was a Jewish pride plank of the movement aimed at articulating Jewish cultural values and history so that they would not fade—as seemed to be happening in places like Bohemia where Irma grew up. *Political Zionism* was far more controversial. Political Zionism was the radical call for an all-Jewish national homeland in Palestine. Zionist thinkers were debating the principles on which such a state could be founded and how to respond to potential backlash against overt Jewish separatism. Political Zionists questioned Jewish assimilation into German culture. *Labor Zionists* rejected religion altogether for Marxist ideals.

Professor Erwin Kolmar was active in the Jewish academic club Bar Kochba but did not call himself a Zionist. He hewed to a competing idea as a Jewish Czech nationalist. He was a follower of parliamentarian Tomáš Masaryk, who envisioned a tolerant democracy in Czech lands that would be free of both religious prejudice and German supremacism. Masaryk was arguing for women's enfranchisement in the Vienna parliament, and would secure their right to vote in 1908—though events delayed voting for another eleven years.

Each line of nationalistic thought—Jewish, Czech, German— was a liberating vision to some of the young intellectuals at university. Irma admired the free-spirited thinking but quickly rebuffed an attempt by Bar Kochba member Oskar Epstein (future husband of her high school friend Elsa Lasch) to recruit her to political Zionism. She was not drawn to any political movement, nor did she feel compelled to focus on Jewishness.

Irma's thoughts focused elsewhere. Her initial chance to vote would come after her twenty-ninth birthday. First, she and Erwin were to be married. The couple walked the old stone streets of Prague, stopping at the cafés in the squares and lingering on the riverbanks to gaze through the mist at the domes, spires, and red tile roofs they loved.

....

Irma's take-charge mother, Karla, insisted that Irma complete a teacher training course, just in case, and a class in modern cook- ing, before she married Erwin. Karla completed Irma's trousseau of monogrammed table linens, a wardrobe of lace collars and cuffs, evening dresses, and a traveling suit—just as Karla would do later for her less academically inclined daughters, Edna and Mela. Erwin had won a fellowship at the University of Oxford, where fellow philologist and Anglo-Saxon language scholar J.R.R. Tolkien was completing his studies at Exeter College. Erwin accepted a teaching job in Trieste at the southern edge of Austria for the few months before their departure. Irma imagined a wonderful life in England.

They married on December 24, 1913, in Budějovice, when she was twenty-three and he twenty-seven. She wore a fairy queen's gown in ivory (never white for a redhead) with lace ruffles weighted by costume pearls at the scoop neckline, and a Spanish lace mantilla. The Kolmars were due in England in September; first they would honeymoon and travel from their base in Trieste.

Irma and Erwin Kolmar's faces are serene, confident, and in love in the photo taken in Trieste in 1914. Through connections in a networked elite, they made friends with eminent bankers and enjoyed concerts and salon conversations in cultured circles. Irma saw the ocean for the first time. They began a library of Tauchnitz editions, English literature in affordable paperback, which they learned to reinforce in chintz binding for display. Irma wrote only a few fragments from that time:

> The crossing from Trieste [to Venice] in one of the notorious storms of the Adriatic was terrifying. The ship tossed up and down and the waves were furious. It was my first sea venture. Everyone was sick. The next day I stood, with Erwin, on the terrace of the St. Mark's Campanile in the golden sunshine. Looking down from one side there was the superb Piazza San Marco with its Renaissance architecture, incomparable harmony, and Byzantine dome. From the other side beyond the canal the magnificent Santa Maria Salute, San Giorgio Maggiore, and the palazzos on the canal; the waters studded with islands—farther out Murano, Burano, and Torcello. Legend has it that the bells of the Campanile go to Rome the week before Easter and are returned on Thursday, blessed by the Pope. I stood next to them when they rang, and will never forget that sound.

....

Back in Prague in the summer of 1914, people were speaking about the Balkans. Irma had paid no attention in 1908 when the Austrian Empire had annexed tiny Bosnia and Herzegovina to clean up the edges where Austrian, Turkish, and Russian influences met. Southern European separatists had caused the Hapsburgs grief before, as when Emperor Franz Josef lost his beloved wife, Elisabeth, to an Italian separatist assassin in 1898. Then, on June 28, 1914, while the Kolmars were still in Trieste, the heir apparent to the Hapsburg throne, Archduke Franz Ferdinand, and his wife, Sophie, were assassinated in Sarajevo, Bosnia, by nineteen-year-old Gavrilo Princip, a Slav national separatist.

Austrian sympathies ran to the Hapsburg family and their loss of a possible successor to Franz Josef. The government sought a way to punish the crime and affirm royal might. Matters were complicated by the Hapsburg monarchy's view that the assassin could not have acted alone. They suspected Russia of meddling in the name of ethnic brotherhood, or Pan-Slavism. Mediators were seeking a quiet diplomatic solution but meanwhile the German Empire, Austria's ally and her rivals Russia, France, and England began planning for war.

Seven months after their wedding, on July 28, 1914, Irma and Erwin were strolling beneath the Gothic towers of Old Town Square when they saw a crowd gather around a town crier mounting some stairs. "Austria declares war on Serbia," he announced, and the crowd erupted in a frenzy of patriotism: The crown prince's death would be avenged, Serbia would be punished for inciting trouble, and honor would be upheld. All would be over in a month. Irma and Erwin stood dumbfounded. Their move to England was just weeks away. A man turned on the silent pair: "What's wrong with you two? You look like you drank vinegar."

Lieutenant Jakob Ehrlich

Home versus Homeland

Up to 1914

Jakob Ehrlich, last seen dancing with Miss Irma Hütter at Deutsches Haus in 1908, sank into his favorite chair at Café Central in Vienna for coffee with whipped cream, apple strudel, and a quiet read of the *New Free Press*. Amidst the bracing black scent of coffee, the clack of porcelain cup on saucer, and the murmur of voices under the high-arched ceiling of ivory and gold, Jakob savored a moment's respite from the driven intensity of political life.

At thirty-six years old in 1913, Jakob stood before hundreds of Jewish delegates from all over the world as vice president of the eleventh World Zionist Congress in Vienna. He had left Budějovice in 1908 to return to Vienna, where he had studied law. There he passed the bar examination, set up his law practice as a barrister a few blocks from Café Central, and plunged into the excitement of realizing the Zionist vision. Client work paid his bills; Zionism consumed the rest of his attention. Urgency, righteousness, and zeal fired up the small cohort of leaders trying to win the hearts and minds of all Jews.

It was time for him to marry, as his dear mother, Fanny, kept reminding him when he visited her at his boyhood home in Moravia. Sometimes Jakob thought of the radiant girl with twenty-four-karat golden hair at Deutsches Haus, thirteen years his junior and an ingenue, and wondered where she was. Back then, Irma had noticed Jakob's six-foot figure, wide-open forehead, and warm, dark eyes that kindled in her presence and thought him striking and glamorous—in an avuncular way. She did not know of his immersion in political Zionism then, nor would her family have approved of its premise: that Jews needed a homeland other than Austria.

Jakob Ehrlich was born in 1877 and grew up poor in a Hasidic Jewish family in Bystřice pod Hostýnem in Moravia, near the province of Galicia (now in Poland) at Austria's eastern edge. Jakob's father, Shmuel (Solomon), was a reclusively religious Hasidic Jew and did not believe in the benefits of a secular higher education. Jakob's elder sisters would never have had a chance to override that belief. But Jakob was the youngest of ten and clever. His mother found a way to send her youngest son to board at Kroměříž so he could attend high school twenty dirt-track miles away.

I have always supposed that Jakob's prodigious sense of responsibility for the Jewish people began with the communal lift that bore him from a rural Jewish enclave, where hunger struck in the spring, to the grandeur of Vienna. He may have benefitted from *essentage*, the tradition of charitable meals from wealthier Jews for students, or contributions from his siblings—not his father. In any case, it was Jews helping poor Jews, and he rose into the 1 percent who made it to university, honor bound to help pay it forward.

During his high school years at Kroměříž, 1882–1886, Jakob and his friends Artur Immerglück and Emil Krassny joined a Jewish student group called Ivria, similar to Bar Kochba, in Prague, to debate Jewish issues. During those years before Zionism, the students read about the treason trial of Captain Alfred Dreyfus in France. Mobs in the land of *liberté, égalité, fraternité* screamed for the innocent man's head, revealing shocking levels of anti-Semitism wrapped in patriotic fervor. The students observed the caution of Vienna's mainstream *New Free Press,* which did not publish editor

Theodor Herzl's thoughts on Dreyfus and anti-Semitism lest they prove inflammatory. They watched Vienna elect a Catholic mayor in 1885, Karl Lueger, who would give the city its dazzling modern infrastructure while playing along with the endemic bigotry in his city: he accepted private Jewish financing but refused to include Jews or ultra-Germans in his administration.

The seal of a former archbishop at the Baroque Archbishop's Palace in Kroměříž, a World Heritage site, illustrates the duality in cameo. Archbishop Kohn was the son of a Jewish-born nobleman who converted to Catholicism. Kohn rose through the ranks of the church on merit. When appointed to high office he chose a seal that incorporated a Star of David, showing pride in the route to his accession. But Austrian Catholic outcry over his Semitic ancestry forced Kohn to step down in 1903, just to keep the peace. Jakob and his friends in Kroměříž concluded that neither loyalty nor integration—not even religious conversion—guaranteed full equal rights to Jews as promised. Austria's constitutional declaration of equal rights for minorities was mired in systemic racism. Jewish people needed to stand up for themselves.

....

Jakob arrived at the University of Vienna for a four-year law degree in 1896, just after Vienna newspaperman Theodor Herzl published the manifesto that launched the Zionist movement, *The Jewish State*. Herzl had hardly identified as Jewish until the uncivilized spectacle of the Dreyfus trial forced a reckoning. High-minded and literary to the point of disconnection, Herzl proposed a mass baptism of Jews as a solution. This ignited fury among religious Jews and a hasty withdrawal by Herzl. Every other ethnicity had or was yearning for a nation of its own. Herzl then suggested that the persistent problem of discrimination against Jewish minorities could be solved for good *only* by creating a separate Jewish state. He declared that a Jewish nation was achievable through states-manship—if Jews would unite in common cause.

The Jewish State begins with an analysis of the vicious cycle that prevents Jews from settling down in safety:

> The Jewish question persists wherever Jews live in appreciable numbers. Wherever it does not exist, it is brought in together with Jewish immigrants. We are naturally drawn into those places where we are not persecuted, and our appearance there gives rise to persecution. This is the case, and will inevitably be so, everywhere, even in highly civilized countries—see, for instance, France—so long as the Jewish question is not solved at the political level.
> —THE JEWISH STATE (Der Judenstaat)

Arriving at the University of Vienna in 1896, Jakob came of age at the precise time and place where Zionism was born. High percentages of Jews in the legal and medical schools incensed ultra-Germans who considered Vienna theirs. On campus where city police could not intervene, German nationalist students baited and beat Jewish students periodically. Fencing was a sport and rite of passage among campus fraternities, which had begun excluding Jews in 1878. A Jewish fraternity called Kadimah took up dueling to defend their honor in the face of slurs. After several clashes and German losses, the German fraternities refused further duels in 1896, saying they would not give satisfaction to those who were beneath them. Refusing a challenge was a dubious way to defend honor, but they made their point. Ultra-German gangs in quasi-military uniforms demonstrated at the gates to curtail Jewish admissions and swarmed into classrooms yelling, *"Juden Raus!"* ("Jews out!"), hauling Jewish-looking students from their seats. Ostracism against Jews was more volatile at the majority-German University of Vienna than in Prague. In Vienna, Irma said, polemics were fashionable, while in Prague she felt a gracious openness to the world among her fellow students.

As in Budějovice, about half of Vienna's population had migrated in from surrounding areas to adopt urban lifestyles. Most visible were the bearded and black-clad Jews escaping poverty in Galicia or Eastern Europe. They stood out as foreign, unhealthy, un-German. Their language, Yiddish, sounded like "dirty German" to Viennese ears. The backlash against Jews that Herzl wrote about—typical to anywhere with a sudden influx of outsiders—was intensified by the German nationalist belief in superior and inferior races. Jakob saw defending them as a matter of equality and justice: a legal problem and an important precedent to set, founded on compassion.

Jakob caught Theodor Herzl's eye as a campus protégé, just when the first World Zionist Congress brought Jewish delegates from all over the world to meet in Basel, Switzerland, in 1897. Herzl's breathtakingly bold re-creation of a parliamentary setting gave enormous dignity to the movement he had sparked. The first World Zionist Congress laid out a sprawling agenda:

Zionism aims at establishing for the Jewish people a publicly and legally assured home in Palestine. For the attainment of this purpose, the Congress considers the following means serviceable:
- Promotion of the settlement of Jewish agriculturists, artisans, and tradesmen in Palestine.
- Federation of all Jews into local or general groups, according to the laws of the various countries.
- Strengthening of the Jewish feeling and consciousness.
- Preparatory steps for the attainment of those governmental grants which are necessary to the achievement of the Zionist purpose.

Why Palestine? The Arab population was adapted to desert conditions and didn't welcome settlers. But Jerusalem had been holy to Jews since their exile two thousand years earlier. Deeply religious Jews would not join the Zionist movement for any other homeland and pragmatic Zionists needed their cooperation. There was no consensus on how peaceful governance between the existing Arab population and Jewish immigrants could be achieved. Incredibly, some delegates made headway with evangelical Christian politicians in Britain who believed that a Jewish return to Zion would unite the world, and conveniently wrest colonial control of Palestine from the Turkish Empire. Zionist leader Chaim Weizmann and other talented statesmen like Nahum Sokolow cultivated the politicians in England.

Zionist congressional delegates met every couple of years to translate ideas into action, then fanned out to constituencies to build the movement. They quickly determined that they needed to engage in local politics for greater visibility and relevance. The movement needed men and women of passion, pragmatism, rhetorical skill, and charm.

Jakob Ehrlich could traverse from village to city and enter deep into the elite halls of justice. He knew the law, and also understood men like his father who cared about spiritual matters over practical ones and viewed life through a theological lens. With fluency in Czech and German, Jakob was at home in most of the empire. He had all the talents the movement needed. An extraordinary convergence had directed the young lawyer to his life's purpose, as though fate were in charge.

....

Among those most difficult to engage were people like Irma and her family: Jews assimilated over time into Austrian culture, such that they felt more aligned with opera-going Europeans than, say, Orthodox ghetto-dwellers from Vladivostok.

The old idea of supporting a few Jews in Palestine was not controversial. It fell neatly into Jewish traditions of philanthropy and communal good deeds. Irma's grandparents, Moritz and Julie Singer, had sent donations to the tiny Jewish colonies, place of last refuge for about five thousand *luftmensch* (air people), spirit-led souls. Philanthropic bankers Lord Rothschild in Britain and Baron de Hirsch of Bavaria had supported them as well. However, the new Zionist proposition of a large-scale Jewish state threatened comfortably assimilated Jews and made them feel conspicuous. Emperor Franz Josef's granting of formal equal rights made assimilated Austrian Jews more comfortable than ever before, and many felt grateful. They feared that calling for a separate homeland would cast dangerous doubt on their patriotism.

The Singer and Hütter families were well-assimilated Bohemians. Irma had loved having a Christmas tree, and a Protestant best friend, and parties with Christian friends. She brushed aside the occasional bigot as unworthy, ill-informed, and ignorant. When Irma or her parents chanted, "Next Year in Jerusalem!" at a Passover Seder, they were honoring a ritual bond, and certainly did not mean it literally. Irma and Erwin wanted to spend their next year in verdant England, not desert Jerusalem.

Jakob, with his legal and rhetorical skills, looked for ways to challenge the assumption that gradual progress would outpace systemic racism. He was one of the authors of a 1911 official Zionist statement directed squarely at getting the attention of complacently integrated Jews, whom they derided as "assimilationists." Jakob's statement read:

Zionism is the destiny of the Jews; assimilation is our dissolution. We are engaged in a life-or-death struggle, in which one of these must triumph. The only compromise between life and death is sickness. Zionism is the extension of national Jewish thought, carried to its logical conclusion. Zionism without a Jewish state is as much an absurdity as a Jewish state without Zionism.

Jakob and Irma—who had rejected Zionist advances in Prague—fell naturally to opposite sides. He was a passionate advocate; she was a natural assimilationist under challenge by Zionists. But controversy was essential to change. Jakob's peers called him respectful, articulate, quick-witted, persuasive. Impeccably dressed with diamond cufflinks and a tie stud, Jakob met with argumentative rabbis, politicians, and youth groups drawn to Marxism, Zionism, or religious purity in varying measure. Each group had their own priorities. Even when working in Budějovice, the heart of assimilated Jewish territory, Jakob inspired people to donate to the Palestine homeland and thereby bring Zionism along.

....

Jewish leadership in Vienna was centered at the Jewish Community Organization or Israelitische Kultusgemeinde (IKG) on Seitenstettengasse near the synagogue. This organization administered funds provided by the Catholic government for Jewish minority schools and social welfare, and raised its own funds by taxing voting members. Established leaders saw their job as taking Jewish problems out of the public eye, where they might offend, and representing Jewish minority interests with a single voice that might be heard by the majority. Jakob and his fellow Zionists made themselves useful by chairing committees at the IKG and providing pro bono legal services, all the while arguing for the Zionist agenda of assertive public confrontation of discrimination.

Vienna's influx of Jewish immigrants consumed Jewish Community resources, but also brought in more Jews vulnerable to harassment on the streets. Vienna's Jewish population grew to 11 percent in three heavily Jewish districts, enough to elect Jakob, then thirty-five, to a seat on the board of directors of the Jewish Community Organization in 1912. He was a rising star in the Zionist movement working toward the vision articulated by the dead founder, Theodor Herzl, in *The Jewish State*:

The Jews who wish for a State will have it.
We shall live at last as free men on our own soil, and die
peacefully in our own homes.
The world will be freed by our liberty, enriched by our
wealth, magnified by our greatness.
And whatever we attempt there to accomplish for our
own welfare, will react powerfully and beneficially for
the good of humanity.

When Jakob could take time away he liked to visit his widowed mother in Moravia, or climb the exhilarating heights of the Rax with his friends Artur Immerglück and Emil Krassny, leaving his worries in the clouds below. Or he'd take his favorite seat at Café Central to reflect, probably unaware that Leon Trotsky might be at another table editing the Bolshevik newspaper *Pravda* in exile. Or that a twenty-four-year-old painter rejected by the Vienna Academy of Fine Arts might be across the room extolling policies of the German mayor Karl Lueger and developing an ideology that would one day be called National Socialism. Jakob Ehrlich, Leon Trotsky, and Adolf Hitler could have been seated at their mutually favorite Café Central on the same day in 1913, amongst habitués swooning over cultural celebrities, tossing out ethnic jokes, and arguing over whether the Wiener schnitzel at Griensteidl's surpassed all contenders.

In the spring of 1914, voices at Café Central rose in debate over whether the assassination of Austria's crown prince Franz Ferdinand ought to lead to war. Austrians eyed the Zionists: would those who wanted a homeland in Palestine fight and die as patriotic Austrians? Jakob, who had maintained his standing in the reserves since his student days, had no doubt. When Austria declared war on Serbia on July 28, 1914—the same day Erwin and Irma looked as though they had drunk vinegar—Jakob began to wrap up his business affairs and let go of community responsibilities. Within a week, on August 4, 1914, Lieutenant Ehrlich volunteered for active duty with the Austrian Royal and Imperial Army.

Lieutenant Erwin Kolmar
called to arms, August 1914

A Damned Foolish Thing
1914–1918

Austrians would recall where they were when the news of war hit on July 28, 1914, in the same indelible way that Americans recall September 11, 2001, or the day John F. Kennedy was shot: a jolt, a pivot, a void. Euphoric crowds in Prague's central square cheered visions of national glory. Irma and Erwin masked their vinegary expressions in public for patriotism's sake and reckoned with dashed dreams. Erwin, a man of military age, would not be permitted to leave the country before things settled down. War meant their move to England was off.

At home in their small apartment on Prague's west bank, Erwin and Irma tried to make sense of the precarious situation. Assassination of an Austrian crown prince demanded punishment, and Imperial Austria could put Serbia in its place without a doubt, but Imperial Russia had promised to defend Serbia in the name of Slavic brotherhood. Military men in Germany, Austria's ally, were looking for a pretense for conquest. Generations later, the cascading events of the next few days still boggle the mind.

Austria declares war on Serbia	July 28, 1914	a punitive expedition
Russia mobilizes	July 30, 1914	but does not declare war
Germany declares war on Russia	August 1, 1914	triggered by Russian mobilization
Germany invades Luxembourg	August 2, 1914	en route to France
Germany declares war on France	August 3, 1914	Germany wants Paris
Germany invades Belgium	August 4, 1914	Belgium has a pact with Britain
Britain declares war on Germany	August 4, 1914	triggered by the pact
Austria declares war on Russia	August 6, 1914	Austria is Germany's ally...

Irma had known Austrian life to be "getting better every day, in every way," as she wrote in her nine-year-old mindset when she heard of the French Revolution. But in the course of a week, the world was at war. Irma had just written her literary thesis on the English classic *Hudibras*, which pilloried the human folly behind religious wars that had bedeviled England and warned the world against such violence. How could Germany, *the land of poets and philosophers*, be marching—unprovoked—upon Paris? How could Austria be at war with the England they so admired? Unimaginably worse, Erwin now faced the prospect of fighting Russia's five-million-man army.

Austria had intended that Serbia's punishment would be a knockout blow followed by formal submission, all to be finished by Christmas. But in a week, the Russian, German, and British Empires had joined. France and Britain declared war on Austria-Hungary on August 12. Imperial Japan would join the fray by the end of the month, with more to follow.

All had been predicted by Otto von Bismarck, the Iron Chancellor who led Germany to world power status but disdained later politicians. At the Congress of Berlin (1878) he had observed:

Europe today is a powder keg and the leaders are like men smoking in an arsenal ... A single spark will set off an explosion that will consume us all . . . I cannot tell you when that explosion will occur, but I can tell you where . . . Some damned foolish thing in the Balkans will set it off.

In August of 1914, eight months after they married, Irma and Erwin pose for a photograph. Soon they would head to the train platform, where he boarded a car bound for Galicia and the Russian front. Irma would celebrate her twenty-fourth birthday on August 28, knowing he was in harm's way.

Dr. Erwin Kolmar, philology scholar and close reader of *Beowulf* and *The Saxon Chronicles*, had always done what was expected of a university man: trained as a military officer, been furloughed into the reserves, received the Crown Jubilee commemorative medal in the emperor's sixtieth year of reign in 1908, and stayed fit. Austria did not maintain a huge standing army and relied instead on reserves, so his deployment was immediate.

Lieutenant Erwin Kolmar of Infantry Regiment 89 appears next in his field uniform: a blue-gray jacket with scalloped pocket flaps and loose trousers wrapped at the calf with puttees. A six-pointed gold star on the collar denotes his rank, a striped ribbon displays his medal, and a drill whistle cord trails from his pocket. Collar and cap bear the regimental colors of claret red, the same red as the trousers packed away for ceremonial spectacle.

Irma would later point to the famous novel *The Good Soldier* Švejk by Jaroslav Hašek as an accurate portrayal of Austrian Czech attitudes. The story revolves around sly Czech conscripts outsmarting incompetent Germanic officers who suspect that disloyal Czechs will shirk duty, surrender, or desert. The soldiers in turn believe that the Austrian high command has no qualms placing non-Germans at the front under impossible conditions. Švejk survives by wily underhandedness, carrying passive resistance to absurd levels. The author was a Czech conscript who felt so mistreated that he deserted to the Russian side.

Keeping his Czech nationalist sympathies to himself, Erwin accepted his military duty. Austrian officials routinely put units under leaders of a different ethnicity to limit fraternization, and so Erwin, a Czech, was put in charge of Galician soldiers. A mutiny before their time had tainted the reputation of Infantry Regiment 89 in the eyes of the Austrian command, and the prior suspicion of the regiment lingered.

Russia's enormous standing army was sweeping westward toward Germany, Austria, and Hungary. A two-hundred-mile eastern front would form from Warsaw in German territory to Przemyśl in the northeastern Austrian province of Galicia (now in Poland) heavily settled with Austrian Jews. Desperate caravans of poor Galician Jews fled west to escape the notoriously rapacious "Russian steamroller" laying waste to eight hundred miles of countryside on their way to the front. Terrified Jews sought safety in Vienna.

Lieutenant Erwin Kolmar took his place as a leader of the 89th infantry regiment (IR89) of the 2nd infantry division of the X Corps in the First Army. Ranking above him was Field Marshal Anton Lipošćak of the 2nd infantry division of the X Corps. Above both was Commander General Hugo Meixner von Zweienstamm, serving under General Viktor Dankl of Austria's First Army, who coordinated strategy with Germany's high command.

By August 20, 1914, Erwin's IR89 was massed with the First Army for battle with Russian forces at Kraśnik by the San River in Galicia where, in ferocious fighting between August 22 and 25, Austria won its first victory. Erwin's regiment pressed north toward Lublin.

Russian armies had new rapid-fire machine guns and long-range artillery acquired after humiliation by Japan in Manchuria in 1904–1905. Austria had not fought a serious war in decades, and the old Mannlicher repeating rifles and short-range Howitzers were no match for Russian weapons. Each attack took an outsized toll on Austrian troops, and especially on infantry officers leading charges directly into enemy fire. The First Army units lost a third of their men in the early disorganized weeks of confrontation, a terrible toll.

Replacements were slow to arrive on the Austrian side, and true to *The Good Soldier Švejk's* theme, one Czech infantry brigade, IR36, nearly mutinied to protest hopeless leadership and desperate conditions. The men were driven back into direct fire by their officers. Russian reinforcements soon forced the entire First Army into retreat, with one hundred thousand taken prisoner according to Russian bulletins.

During October and early November, General Dankl's outnumbered army spread out along the San and Vistula rivers to prepare for a new offensive near Krakow. The weather turned cold and rainy. Dysentery, typhoid, and cholera added to the misery. Fighting began on November 17 and raged on for the next week. X Corps lost another third of its fighting men, a toll so severe that Dankl asked the high command to reduce the First Army's burden of attack. Erwin's beleaguered IR89, about twenty miles north of Krakow near a village called Sułoszowa, were told to hold their position defensively while adjacent units attacked. Irma was staying with Erwin's parents at their home in Plzeň (Pilsen) when they received notice: as of November 28, 1914, Erwin was missing, presumed dead.

She could not accept it. Austria was so overwhelmed by fighting on many fronts that records were often wrong. Irma wrote only a few words down on paper about this time:

> Ernst Wiesl (from Klatovy) became a friend. He studied in Prague. He was with his regiment in Plzeň in December 1914 when the news of Erwin's death in the Battle of Sułoszowa, where he himself had been wounded, spread. He hobbled on crutches to the apartment of my parents-in-law to comfort me and told me not to give up hope.

There had been such confusion in the Austrian army that misinformation was the order of the day. It was the last time I saw him. After his wounds had been healed he returned to the Russian front, where he was killed. My brother-in-law Fritz Werner [sister Edna's husband] was made a prisoner of war in the Battle of Sułoszowa on November 25, 1914, and spent six years in Siberia Beresovka, later Vladivostok.

Irma did not give up hope. She prayed. She summoned him with her heart. He did not come. Disbelieving, insane with grief, Irma went searching for Erwin. She made her way to Poland against all advice, hired a cart and driver, and rode to Sułoszowa in freezing winter weather. The line of fighting had moved on. Irma saw mortar shell holes that could have swallowed whole groups of men, graves, and the devastating debris of war. A few villagers saw a ghostly widow searching in deranged solitude for her lover. Her memoir fell wordless for four years.

....

Nearby along the Eastern Front, Lieutenant Jakob Ehrlich of IR1 fought on, surviving the first months when casualties were highest. We find him in his blue-gray uniform with the distinctively scalloped pockets, and in belted sheepskin great coat and high boots near a timber-reinforced trench blanketed in snow. His war record—medals of bronze and silver for specific actions, and gold for overall value—trace First Army movements:

1914–15 near Lublin and near Krakau (Russia, now Poland) . . . in recognition of dutiful behavior before the enemy . . .

1916 near Turya/Sepanow (Russia, now Ukraine) . . . bravely and without fear, organized the Brigade under heavy artillery fire when they had no telephone or other means to connect.

Perhaps he was a popular commander, with his power to convey understanding and words that could inspire and motivate.

Fighting on the Eastern Front died down in 1917, when the Bolshevik Revolution distracted the Russians. While the Great War raged on along the Western Front, German troops occupied Russia as far east as Odessa, and Jakob was reassigned to serve as a lawyer for the military court. Five young Jewish soldiers in Odessa, one the son of a prominent Zionist, were accused of treason in a court case that seemed to echo that of Alfred Dreyfus in France. Jakob's defense saved the young men, raised his profile in the Zionist world, and reinforced Zionist resolve to secure a homeland for persecuted Jews.

Russia's breakdown and collapse of the Eastern Front coincided with a low ebb in Austria. The eighty-six-year-old emperor Franz Joseph died in November of 1916 and a new emperor was named, but the future of the empire seemed uncertain. With hope for an end to the war in sight, Czech statesmen Tomáš Masaryk and Edvard Beneš lobbied the Allies to recognize peaceful Czech aspirations and carve out a Czech nation after the war.

....

From ages twenty-four to twenty-eight, Irma lived her grief. Food grew scarcer as Austria's defeat grew near; Irma loathed beans and turnips ever after. She bore a crushing suspicion that Erwin's unit had been sacrificed to the front—*Soldier Švejk* style—for an earlier generation's noncompliance in the ranks. Her sister Edna worried about her husband, Fritz Werner, taken prisoner in the battle that killed Erwin, and surviving on air-dropped Red Cross packages in Siberia. Irma forced herself to work as a tutor, then as a teacher of art history at the boys' middle school in Prague, and she took a little bit of solace from the bright eyes of young students. Austria needed translators in Turkish, so she took up the call to study the difficult language.

America's entry into the war in April 1917 helped bring it to a conclusion within a year. Germany and Imperial Austria were the losers. On a trip to America in 1918, Czech statesman Tomáš Masaryk would win support for a Czech state from American president Woodrow Wilson, whose principle of *self-determination* for nations would dismantle the Austrian Empire and replace it with sovereign nations. The weakened empire would lose 60 percent of her former territory, becoming what some called a head with no body.

....

The Czech janitor in Irma's apartment building in Prague observed the sad, beautiful widow come and go from her teaching job. She greeted him in Czech when they passed in the hallway, and the lonely man saw in her hazel eyes a lady in need of rescue. He knocked on her door one evening, hat in hand. To her utter astonishment, he fell straight to his knees and offered his hand in marriage. But what could the simple man know of her education, her aspirations, the vividness of her love? How could old-fashioned kindness ever be enough for Irma? With her door gently closed behind him, she laughed at the solemn proposal and cried for herself. Irma realized something important: she had not made plans beyond grief. When asked by her grandchildren about Erwin, Irma's chest would heave. "Ach, *that* was a love!"

In honor of Erwin Kolmar, the man who was dead before he could become my grandfather, let us engage our imaginations in a few degrees of separation. He is my honorary ancestor. Had he made it to England with Irma after the war, would he have discussed the Anglo-Saxon language of *Beowulf* with J.R.R. Tolkien at Oxford, and cofounded the Inklings literary society there, and befriended fellow member C. S. Lewis? Ah, but I would not be here to celebrate that. The Anglo-Saxon amalgam that is me would not have been born. In Imperial Austria, Jews had been meeting their mates within a radius of fifty miles or less for hundreds of years. Erwin Kolmar and I may even share some DNA.

Irma's University of Vienna pass, 1918

Self-Determination

1918–1923

January 1918: Austrian forces trickled home from the East while wartime ally Germany fought on in France. Terms of an armistice were under discussion, though postwar settlements would take more than a year to work out. American president Woodrow Wilson proposed *Fourteen Points* to ground peace negotiations, including point number ten: "The peoples of Austria-Hungary, whose place among the nations we wish to see safeguarded and assured, should be accorded the freest opportunity of autonomous development."

In other words, the Austrian Empire was finished, but Austria would survive as a nation under a democratic principle Wilson called *self-determination*. "National aspirations must be respected," Wilson said, meaning that cultural and ethnic affinities would define future states. In October of 1918, Erwin's dream of an independent Czechoslovakia would come true, and long-term advocate Tomáš Masaryk would be elected president. But that was neither consolation nor inspiration to Irma. Czech independence had been Erwin's vision, not hers. No death certificate confirmed it, but Erwin was gone.

Alone and lonely, Irma had her own form of *self-determination* to consider. Most young women would choose to be close to family. She did not want to live in grief near Erwin's parents in Plzeň, nor could she consider going back to sleepy Budějovice with her parents. Her beloved Prague was the city of lost happiness and would belong to the new Czechoslovakia. Goosed into action by a marriage proposal from a janitor, a complete stranger, Irma thought of the Germanic cultural capital she had visited just once as a teen: Vienna. She had no friends there, but to stay where she was would be to surrender to victimhood. She summoned her pride.

....

With Armistice on November 11, 1918, a temporary country called the *Republic of German-Austria* was declared. That shrunken post-Empire Austria planned to unite with the Weimar Republic of Germany, so that the two wartime allies would become one expanded German Reich. Ethnic Germans along the German–Czech borderlands hoped to join as well.

But Wilson's principle of self-determination did not apply fully to Austrian Germans. Britain and France thought that German military aggression should not be rewarded with any territorial gains, and they did not want Germany too powerful. Final treaty terms forbade German unification for twenty years at least. The *Republic of German-Austria* had to drop "German" from its name, and a volatile sense of wronged brotherhood—strong pan-German feelings that had been in play all along—slipped underground to fester.

Postwar Vienna still had its imposing parliament buildings designed to project cold imperial power over sixty million people, but it ruled over a mere six million. On Vienna's grand circular boulevard, the Ringstrasse, the Vienna State Opera house where Mozart and Da Ponte's *Don Giovanni* had played for the 1869 opening and Gustav Mahler had directed the Vienna

Philharmonic stood dormant and in need of repair. Palatial Ring-strasse homes like those of the international grain merchants and art connoisseurs, the Ephrussi family, still traced the line of the old city wall. Intellectuals and artists like Sigmund Freud and composer Arnold Schoenberg went back to work in a city of past glories.

Irma had seen Imperial Vienna once in 1906 when visiting her aunt Ida von Ptak, daughter of her grandma Julie's brother, Lippmann Kohner of the Imperial and Royal Jewelers:

I

When I was about sixteen, Aunt Ida and Uncle Alfred von Ptak invited me to spend Easter vacation with them. He was a colonel who later became general [and presided at a fort called Terezín or Theresienstadt of later note]. I was so excited to go. Austria was a Catholic country and its capitol famous for ceremonies and pageantry. On Holy Friday, Emperor Franz Joseph I proved his humility before the Savior by washing the feet of a selected beggar who had been scrubbed and disinfected first. Easter Sunday was a solemn procession of the Imperial Court to Stephansdom. The Archbishop of Vienna led the procession, followed by high clergy in their gold and silver brocade vestments. The members of the Imperial Court followed. Their Majesties were absent, as the Emperor, born in 1830, was too old to attend. The Empress Elisabeth stayed mostly in Corfu, an island in the Aegean, after the suicide of their only son, Crown Prince Rudolf. Next in the procession came all the archdukes in their resplendent uniforms and feathered helmets, followed by the duchesses, princes, and princesses, and high-ranking military and government representatives. The night was watched in reverence by crowds of Viennese and spectators from all parts of the Empire.

Vienna in 1918 could not have its former imperial pomp and panache, but the music palaces, museums, and broad promenades promised a cosmopolitan life. And once again, Irma landed by happenstance—not by political choice—in the Zionist fold, just as she had at Charles University in Prague with her choice to dine with Zionist not Orthodox Jews.

The link to Zionism was biblical scholar Dr. Zwi Perez Chajes, who had been promoted from Trieste to become chief rabbi in Vienna. He had warmed to Zionism after Erwin and Irma knew him in Trieste, and was an important unifying figure in the movement. Through Rabbi Chajes, Irma would meet Zionist women who would become her role models not for their politics but for their philanthropic vigor.

We return to Irma, who turned twenty-eight on August 28, 1918.

2

I had to make a new start. I had taught at the trade school in Plzeň and built up a considerable private practice teaching English and art appreciation. Someone suggested I apply for a position at Dr. Bloch's Wäring District Girls' Gymnasium [academic high school founded by an outspoken and progressive Jewish rabbi and statesman] in Vienna at 18 Gentzgasse. To my amazement, I got an interview immediately and was accepted. I had to inform the directors of the schools in Plzeň of my decision shortly before the beginning of the new academic year, which caused them great inconvenience. They were very gracious about it, and I received charming and cordial letters of well-wishing for my new life.

I spent two weeks at Mayrhofen in the Alps with my mother before venturing to Vienna. There were fierce battles on the Italian front south of Mayrhofen in the Dolomites, and I was warned not to stray when hiking alone at Hintertux as there were desperate deserters. One day, walking to our hotel with my mother, I felt sick. She couldn't walk fast, so I rushed alone to reach our room with my last strength and fell unconscious inside the door. I was violently sick all night long but improved the next day. Though I didn't know it at the time, that attack provided me with some immunity during the terrible siege of Spanish flu in the winter of 1919. [The 1918–1920 epidemic killed two million people in Europe, especially young adults under age forty, including returning troops.]

I arrived in Vienna in the desperate fall of 1918 [time of the short-lived Republic of German-Austria], alone in the strange big city, unsure of myself, needing all my courage and resolve to start a new life.

There was the horrifying collapse of the monarchy, that drab day in front of the Parliament, the shooting and stampede over falling bodies, when someone seized my hand and dragged me into a house on the Ringstrasse where some people found refuge. [An unidentified explosion on November 12, 1918, caused a panic and deaths by trampling.] Then came the influenza. Everybody was sick. I had a slight attack, rather late, after lots of people I knew died.

At the end of the war Vienna was a sad city. Her population was starving, food supplies exhausted, no fuel. Inside of my active life, I couldn't get rid of a deep-seated foreboding. In discussions I used to stubbornly insist that Austria was doomed—truncated as she was, overrun by alien speculators, without the industries and resources of the provinces; with Vienna, the easygoing capital of the previous empire, impoverished and starving.

I had no family I could rely upon [not being close to her maternal grandmother's Kohner-side relatives at that point]. Yet that year in Vienna was successful professionally and socially. I had an enormous number of private students and met many prominent and interesting people. Through introduction by Dr. Chajes, the beloved and famous chief rabbi I knew from Trieste, I met Erna Patak and the Zionists who gathered at her villa. I met bankers and financiers at the homes of Robert Fanta [banker introduced by a connection in Budějovice] and Milan Herrmann; and artists and aristocracy at the home of [cultured industrialist] Roberto Metzger, who continued his friendship from Trieste.

I saw alarming signals [of instability]. At Robert Fanta's, or the lovely villa of Irma and Milan Herrmann on Jordan Street, we heard chamber music by kerosene stove and candlelight, and ate rutabaga and carrots. Meanwhile I saw lavish entertainment in the enormous flat of my Romanian pupils on the Stephansplatz, opposite the dome and gargoyles and bells of the cathedral. Their father was a stock speculator [one of the "alien speculators" widely viewed as a profiteering scourge on the vulnerable city]. They always set a huge lunch table with silver and precious china and delicacies for twelve to twenty guests so that he and his business associates could stop by casually on their return from the Bourse. Within a couple of years, they had all disappeared from Vienna.

3

Erna Patak was a wealthy divorcée, an enthusiastic Zionist driven by her desire to help the Jewish people. She ran a convalescent home, a beautiful, spacious place with terraces and gardens opposite the Türkenschanz Park. Her patients were all kinds of Zionist intellectuals whom she befriended. One of her chief concerns was arranging transportation of undernourished Jewish children to Holland.

She spent a lot of time helping poor Jewish youngsters who arrived in Vienna from the eastern provinces, particularly Galicia, whom she tried to place in trade schools. [Jews from Galicia fled to Vienna in mortal fear of Russian troops during the war, and from local (then Polish) hostility in the aftermath. After the Bolshevik Revolution in Russia in 1917 and its backlash, anti-Semites continued to target Jews as suspected Bolsheviks.]

Her house was run by an efficient housekeeper as she herself was always on the go. She was indefatigable. I think she never had a paying patient. People waited in the foyer at her clinic from the early morning hours. On her arthritic legs she was always on the lookout to find supporters and raise funds. I lived in the same neighborhood [near Türkenschanz Park, a nice residential area near Dr. Bloch's school] and was often her guest. On Sundays and holidays when she was at home there were numerous guests. She seemed to know many celebrities—people of influence and means, and civic authorities.

Sometime in late winter I was asked over for dinner. There were two newcomers, Mr. Pine and Mr. Cailles, delegates of the American Joint Distribution Committee. They were there to study conditions and needs of the Jewish community in this difficult time and recommend help, and became frequent visitors. [Her English may have been useful.]

4

At the spring elections for town council in Vienna, Jakob Ehrlich received great publicity. There was lots of talk about him since he became a city councilor candidate as a Zionist for the second district [Leopoldstadt] in the new labor government of Vienna. I heard of him at Erna Patak's house and told her I had known a Dr. Jakob

Ehrlich in my hometown when I was a schoolgirl. "*Ja, das ist ihr Dr. Ehrlich,*" she said. ("Yes, *that's your* Dr. Ehrlich.")

I met Jakob Ehrlich at Erna Patak's. He had returned from Odessa only in January 1918 [after being detained for months by Bolsheviks and robbed of all he carried on the train]. Dr. Ehrlich came ever more frequently when I was there. They began to tease me.

Shortly before my vacation started in June 1919, he asked me to join him on a climb on the Rax [in the Alps]. But a few days before the scheduled departure I called the date off and informed him I was leaving for Budějovice and would not return to Vienna. I did not know yet what I was going to do [she made up a white lie because she felt uncertain]. I only knew this Rax hike would be decisive [he might propose] and I wanted to escape.

························

Yes, that was *her* Dr. Ehrlich, as Erna Patak had put it.

I'd wager that Jakob's close friends Dr. Chajes and Erna Patak conspired as well-motivated matchmakers can do. How else would Jakob have known exactly when to find Irma in Erna's garden, such that the busy candidate "came ever more frequently when I was there"? Though smitten and much delayed in marriage prospecting by the war, Jakob Ehrlich knew he had been refused when mountain-loving Irma backed out of a trip to the Rax.

Irma's summer in placid Budějovice sufficed to turn her head around. She wanted very much to go back to her stimulating life and good job in Vienna. Jakob had grown all the more striking since the time he had danced with her at Deutsches Haus in Budějovice, his forehead a little broader for the receding hairline and his darkly intense eyes warmer. Her friends had teased her for good reason: she had been flirting back.

I imagine the conversation that summer with her mother and sisters, who remembered the handsome lawyer Ehrlich from his time in Budějovice. Irma's heart had been Erwin's. Would he want her to be a sad widow forever, a casualty of war? The war had wiped out thousands of marriageable men. Was she not flattered to have the attention of a man like Jakob? Did she not find him fine? Was she not seeing nobility in Zionism, through her friends Erna Patak and Rabbi Chajes? Was she really going to turn down a decorated veteran, a university man, a member of government, a pillar of Vienna's Jewish community? Meanwhile, her sister Edna waited in agony for news of her husband working his way raggedly home from imprisonment in Siberia—she would wait until 1921—while her sister Meli, twenty-six, was still without a suitable mate.

Irma returned to her teaching in Vienna in the autumn of 1919 and took classes at the University of Vienna: Heroic Sagas; French Syntax; Chaucer; Nineteenth-Century English, and Spanish and French art. A sequence of personal notes passed between the rejected Jakob and hesitant Irma. Each letter was finely inked in formal German with Gothic letters as spiky as steeples with curls looping out like gargoyles. I could hardly decipher them. Among the *thee*s and *thou*s, and fancy capital letters, Irma was persuading Jakob not to give up on her. I imagine his doubts: If she backed away from him once, would she do so again? He would never be rich, he was thirteen years her senior, and his Zionist commitment would absorb him nights and weekends as before. Could she tolerate that? Irma felt she just needed time to adjust. They were matched in education and sophistication; he would accomplish *more, not less* with her by his side. She wanted their child, if a woman over the age of thirty would still be able to conceive.

....

And when romance bloomed, and they knew they would marry, they could not—yet. Like hundreds of others widowed in wartime confusion, Irma first needed a death certificate to be free.

Erwin Kolmar's certificate was issued in Prague on September 30, 1921, nearly seven years after his death, when authorities were documenting best guesses. The certificate states that Professor Erwin Kolmar of the Mosaic faith (of Moses) was killed in battle on November 28, 1914, citing reports from 1915 and 1916 suggesting that no one survived to say how it happened. The men just vanished.

Three months later, Irma and her parents shivered in rainy darkness waiting for Jakob to emerge from a political meeting that overflowed into the evening because, even on his wedding day, Councilor Ehrlich would not let it pass when a fellow member referred to Viennese Jews as "parasites" and "foreigners." As if to set a precedent for how politics would intervene in their lives, Jakob showed up late to his own wedding. A small ceremony united them on December 21, 1921, at the Jewish Community Organization hall on Seitenstettengasse, near the synagogue. She was thirty-one; he was forty-four.

....

You can go gaze at the elegant bay window of the third-floor apartment at number 22 Weimarer Street in the Währing District of Vienna, just a few blocks away from Türkenschanz Park. The building ran deep, with the parlor in front, bedroom and Jakob's study in the middle, kitchen at the back with a child's bedroom overlooking the Eisenmann & Sohn paper-packaging factory in the courtyard. Irma decorated with light-loving white linen curtains for summer and heavy green brocade silk drapes against the winter cold. A large Biedermeier cabinet with glass shelves on top displayed family heirlooms. Add a complete set of red-and-white patterned Meissen porcelain dishes, a wedding gift perhaps, and multiple sets of embroidered table linens. Tuck in some lofty eiderdown bedding with red-and-white ticking edged in lace. Put in red bentwood chairs and table from the Vienna Workshop artisans to brighten the foyer. Layer in the smells of goulash stewing and Dobos torte baking in the 1920s and 1930s, and you probably have it about right.

Within a year, Irma knew she was pregnant. Mindful of general custom as well as Jakob's insistence that a child needs a mother close, she gave up her teaching job. Paul Ehrlich was born on February 26, 1923, the Viennese son of two Czech-born parents. A Czech couple, Rosa and Sylvester Mazura, occupied the ground-floor apartment. Sylvester was the foreman of the Eisenmann & Sohn factory in the courtyard, with its machine for folding patented fans of single-dose powdered medicine packets. Rosa was happy to earn a little by helping Mrs. Ehrlich and caring for baby Paul upstairs. A photo captures a merry-eyed Irma holding plump baby Paul in her lap. She wears the expression she later displayed with grandbabies that came with a soundtrack: the song "Away to the City."

Irma and Paul, 1923

Zionist Statesman in Vienna

1920s–1933

―•――――――•―

We leave Irma and Paul nesting at 22 Weimarer Street and follow Jakob downtown to Café Central for coffee with sweet whipped cream. If we then walk the few blocks to the Ehrlich, Immerglück, and Smitka law office at 9 Helfersdorfer Street, we find a few clients coming and going amidst a buzzing hive of Zionist activity. Jakob had returned from the war to a fresh new republic in Austria *and* Britain's promise of a Jewish homeland in Palestine. He and his Zionist colleagues had the amazing opportunity to set precedent for fair treatment of Jews in both places. In the early 1920s Jakob was building a family, a law practice, a Zionist voice on the city council, and a network of support for Jewish Palestine—all at once.

The Balfour Declaration that came during the war in 1917 was *only* a promise at first, a letter to the Jewish community in Lord Rothschild's name from the British foreign secretary Lord Balfour, the Christian Zionist. It was the result of emphatic lobbying by Chaim Weizmann and others while Britain was staking out postwar colonies. All questions of actual governance—such as how to reconcile promises to Arabs and Jews—were postponed. Brief in words but colossal in implications, the letter read:

His Majesty's government view with favour the estab-
lishment in Palestine of a national home for the Jewish
people, and will use their best endeavours to facilitate the
achievement of this object, it being clearly understood that
nothing shall be done which may prejudice the civil and
religious rights of the existing non-Jewish communities
in Palestine, or the rights and political status enjoyed by
Jews in any other country.

By 1920, the first British high commissioner for the future
mandate, Sir Herbert Samuel, was in the newly carved-out
territory of Palestine trying to balance Arab and Jewish demands
for self-determination. Jewish leaders bought land from Arabs
and began to build infrastructure. Worldwide Zionists directed
Jewish donations to help settle refugees displaced by the war and
continued to lobby in Britain for Jewish interests.

....

Tens of thousands of Jews had fled to Vienna from Galicia,
Austria's erstwhile province under Polish governance after the
war. Their presence in Vienna aroused German nationalist senti-
ment in the same way large numbers of immigrants of uncertain
status have in the US, or wherever a sudden influx is visibly different from the mainstream. Vienna's fragile new government,
German and Catholic as before, worried about the economic and
social cost. They decided to limit citizenship to those living in the
city at the end of the war. The selective intent of the law was clear.
Immigrants from Czech or Hungarian lands blended in a way
Jewish refugees from Eastern Europe did not. Squads scoured
Jewish neighborhoods for poor Galician Jews without proof of
prior residence. But Poland's Catholic government refused to
accept Galician deportees from Vienna. The League of Nations
intervened, forcing Poland to admit them—an unhappy outcome
for all, since the Jews did not feel safe where they were unwanted.

Jakob filed lawsuits for Jews desperately petitioning to confirm citizenship status in Vienna.

At first Irma just watched admiringly as her Zionist and matchmaking friend Erna Patak joined up with an international network of women focused on helping such displaced Jews. Irma wrote:

> Erna Patak became president of Women's International Zionist Organization (WIZO, Austrian chapter) with headquarters in London. WIZO assisted emigrant women once they arrived in Palestine, teaching and training them for pioneer work and taking care of their children. There were also the young refugees from Eastern countries who arrived at her house daily seeking help. She placed them in artisan schools to prepare for constructive work in the land of their choice. She was active on the committee to establish a kibbutz in Vienna for agricultural training to send proud young Jews to build up their barren, old, neglected homeland by the sweat of their brows. The kibbutz was established in the early fall of 1922.

Armed with eloquence and purpose, Jakob Ehrlich took on the many roles of a statesman. When the 14th World Zionist Organization conference opened at Vienna's concert hall in August of 1925, Jakob stood at the podium to welcome hundreds of delegates from all parts of the world. Anti-Jewish German nationalists protested their presence outside. Embarrassed by the disorder, the city responded by assigning city police to escort the organization's president, Chaim Weizmann, and his wife through a violent mob. Jakob entered the hall with a phalanx of Zionist youth protecting him from bodily harm. Jakob's inaugural address focused squarely on mission and progress, highlighting the symbolic laying of a cornerstone for a Hebrew University in Jerusalem:

Despite a five-year war, despite the terrible postwar period, despite emergencies and deaths, this plan was carried out, and if the torch which was ignited in Jerusalem is carried forward, as the hearts of all humanity pray, to be one in love and aspirations, then the Fourteenth Congress will take a place of honor in our movement. So I hope that this, our Fourteenth Congress, will also be blessed with success and that its deliberations lay the path forward to become a free people among free peoples, for our own happiness and the welfare of all mankind.

....

My grandfather Jakob's lyrical phrasing lifts me like a chorus and reminds me of Martin Luther King: love, bless, pray ... freedom, happiness, honor. I recognize his last words from the original Zionist manifesto and think, *Yes, he was leading a movement of people united by a higher cause.* In the audience were rabbis, diplomats, and freedom-fighting militants grappling with fundamental differences on how to build a state: Did Jews need to take up arms to defend themselves against Arabs, or should they trust British rule and diplomacy to settle affairs in an agreed-upon form of government? What sort of government could rule fairly over both Jews and Arabs in one state, or should there be two? What role would religion play, when Judaism itself was fractured? Zionism's divisions today reflect all the battles of those early days. One hundred years later, religious fundamentalists still spar bitterly with moderates, ultranationalists, and militants. The early Zionists had one thing in common: they believed that Jews belonged together as an ethnicity as well as a religious group, however fractured, and so they deserved their own nation—just as Germans and Czechs deserved theirs.

Jakob could not always win support for confronting prejudice within Vienna, but he carried the Zionist Congress themes to his constituents so persuasively that the whole Jewish community voted to give to Palestine annually, like a tithe. In gratitude,

Zionists honored his name by inscribing it in the golden book of the Jewish National Fund, the Keren Kayemeth, for outstanding contributions to the Jewish state. Then, in 1927 the community threw a glittering party to celebrate Jakob's fiftieth year, thirty of which had been devoted to helping the Jewish people. Irma stood radiantly by his side at the Jewish Community Organization hall—right where she'd married him six years earlier.

Middle-class Viennese Jews like Irma were aware of an undercurrent of Catholic antagonism toward Jews but felt little prejudice in their daily lives. The mainstream *New Free Press* sought middle ground by publishing literary essays by Jewish writers and avoiding content that inflamed the feelings of German supremacists. A rabidly anti-Semitic press existed, as did a partisan Jewish press focused on minority concerns. Irma had always had both Jewish and Gentile friends and so was typical in paying little attention to the politicized fringes. She had seen ugly incidents—like the time she visited her Protestant school friend Marie von Kohoutek in Germany in 1916 and heard German soldiers jeering "draft dodger" at Jews—a bitter irony given that Erwin had died fighting for Austria while Marie's brother held a privileged position administering a private estate for a nobleman that exempted him from battle. She locked the memory away in a compartment. In everyday life, like her parents before her, she protected Paul from awareness of what she saw as a misguided underclass of hostile anti-Semites.

As promised, Irma accepted Jakob's many absences and took care of Paul at home. Rosa Mazura from the flat downstairs stepped in as nanny when Irma headed out in silk and diamond earrings for a night with Jakob at the opera. Paul learned German manners from Struwwelpeter, the wild-haired storybook kid whose minor misdeeds bring disasters, and by laughing off the stiff old maxim that children should *stumm wie ein Fisch* [go silent as a fish] at the dinner table. He rode the giant Ferris wheel in Prater Park, was reprimanded by a policeman for picking up a chestnut on the grass instead of staying on the sidewalk, scraped his knees falling off his scooter on visits to friends, and memorized streetcar routes. Number 38 led to Grinzing and a walk in the hills over the blue Danube. Paul, with his big-rimmed, thin, and sensitive ears, received his first violin lessons. He adopted the tune of the streetcar man's singsong station calls as his musical warm-up.

Irma saw her sister Melanie marry a wealthy businessman, Rudi Brok, in 1922, and shared sister Edna's relief when her husband, Fritz Werner, straggled home from Siberia on foot. Paul met his grandparents, Karla and Hans, in Budějovice; and later cousins Lilly, Hannah, and John Werner in Prague; and Heini and Rudi Brok in Vodňany, Czechoslovakia.

·····················

To be a Zionist on the Vienna Municipal Council was to be conspicuous. Jews were a 10 percent minority in a Vienna that was 80 percent Germanic and Catholic. Jakob represented Leopoldstadt, where 30 percent of Vienna's Jews lived, many of them poor immigrants who lived as though segregated from the mainstream. By promising to hold the city to its constitutional guarantee of equal rights for all, Jakob took on the dual challenges of confronting prejudice and uniting a diversity of Jewish opinions behind him.

Anti-Semitism was part of the Catholic clergy's mindset, and so latent in the Catholic country. Turn-of-the-century mayor Karl Lueger expressed the common view that Jews were drawn to communism, and warned them not to be disloyal. In a speech in 1905 Lueger said, "We in Vienna are anti-Semites, but we certainly weren't made to commit murder and manslaughter. Yet should the Jews threaten our fatherland, we will know no mercy either."

Zionists knew to expect a measure of intolerance from mainstream Christian Germans, who disguised their reflexive prejudice but respected the law, and they knew of the ultra-German supremacist fringe who drummed for boycotts, quotas, and expulsions of Czechs, Jews, non-Germans. Within the Jewish community, they faced opposition from anti-religion Marxists and those who objected to secular politics. Jakob's greatest opposition came from a much larger set of comfortably assimilated Jews who objected to airing Jewish problems in public. This group thought that calling attention to Jewish otherness was socially and politically suicidal because it undermined their goal of integration. Zionists called them "assimilationists" and considered them to be complacent and passively complicit in perpetuating unfair treatment of Jews.

One assimilationist was Walther Rathenau, a business tycoon and diplomat who served Germany's Weimar Republic as foreign minister. In a memoir, he expressed his assimilated Jewish identity in this way: "I am a German of Jewish origin. My people are the German people, my home is Germany, my faith is German faith, which stands above all denominations (*An Deutschlands Jugend*, 1918).

Chaim Weizmann, president of the World Zionist Organization, tried to convince the eminent statesman that he was wrong to be confident in German discernment, but failed to win him over to Zionism. In his 1949 autobiography, *Trial and Error*, Weizmann summarized their difference in perspective:

> His attitude was, of course, all too typical of that of many assimilated German Jews; they seemed to have no idea that they were sitting on a volcano. They believed quite sincerely that such difficulties as admittedly existed for German Jews were purely temporary and transitory phenomena, primarily due to the influx of East European Jews, who did not fit into the framework of German life, and thus offered targets for anti-Semitic attacks. The "real" German Jew would be immune from, above all that. . . .

German Jewish author Jakob Wassermann described what he and other assimilationists thought of Yiddish-speaking refugees from Eastern European shtetls, reflecting thoughts Irma kept to herself as Jakob's wife:

> If I saw a Jew from Poland or Galicia, if I talked to him and tried to probe into him to comprehend his way of thinking and living, he could definitely touch or surprise me, or move me to compassion and sadness, but I certainly didn't feel a sense of brotherhood or even relatedness. In everything he said and breathed, he was a total stranger to me, and when there was no human–individual symbiosis, I even found him repulsive.

Jakob took the floor at the municipal council as a man of the law: rational, bold, suave. He confronted denials of soft discrimination by laying out facts: Jews were not getting government jobs proportional to their number. Guilds should admit Jews, regardless of past tradition. Jews deserved governmental allocations proportionate to those given to Christian institutions such as schools and churches. Citizenship should not be decided on the basis of race or religion, and the assembly should not tolerate casual reference to Jews as "foreigners," or worse, "parasites." Laws should be made and enforced fairly, and not cynically target Jews. He reminded the assembly of countless contributions to the national identity by Jews like Gustav Mahler, Sigmund Freud, Arnold Schoenberg, Arthur Schnitzler, Stefan Zweig, and so on.

Jakob listened as intently as he spoke and shone as a moderator among Jewish factions. Gradually Zionists won favor in the quasi-governmental Jewish Community Organization, the social welfare and political interest group previously dominated by middle-class assimilationists. With Zionism's success, Jakob's burden of work only increased. On top of his private practice and city council work, he took on the unpaid presidency of the Austrian Zionist Federation and chairmanship of voluntary committees for the community: pro bono legal defense, immigrant issues, and youth organizations. After years of proving themselves in word and deed, Zionists won a majority with twenty-one of the thirty-six seats in the Jewish Community Organization. In 1932, Jakob's old office mate Desider Friedmann was elected community president. Zionists had won Vienna.

Much of the compassion and persistence Jakob gave to public service for the Jewish people came at the cost of family time. When Irma and Paul went to the Alps for three weeks, Jakob joined them for one. When the family strode the hills outside Vienna on a Sunday afternoon, a business colleague might be in tow. At the age of nine in 1932, Paul would have liked more time with his father, but he also loved time with his friends as he grew tall on Wiener schnitzel and Sacher torte. Irma had more free time as a result. When she was not volumizing a dense hazelnut torte with whipped cream or seeing that Paul got to violin lessons, she began stopping at Jakob's office to type in German, Czech, French, and English and generally make herself useful.

....

In 1933, at the age of fifty-five, Jakob left the daily struggles behind to take a look at what his life's devotion to the Zionist quest had produced. Backed by his capable wife and ten-year-old music-loving son at home, in the company of dear old friends Emil Krassny and Artur Immerglück, Jakob made a pilgrimage to Jerusalem. Sailing with the wind on board the vessel to Palestine, with the wide sea as his horizon, Jakob had precious time for quiet reflection. Millions before him had suffered and persevered; his father, Shmuel, had called for Jerusalem each year of his life in the Seder's ritual mourning for the lost homeland; Theodor Herzl had died after sparking the movement; and he, Jakob, was leading his people to the Promised Land.

Palestine was still a colony under a British governor while the hope for a self-ruled Jewish state still shimmered in the distance. The Jewish population had swelled from 90,000 in 1923 to

235,000 in 1933, from 10 to 20 percent of the whole. Europeans migrated in as pioneers braving disease, hostility, and hardship in parched desert and insect-ridden marshlands. Arab objections were growing. British leaders had to limit entry visas as they searched for the elusive formula that would make Arabs and Jews live in peace. Yet water systems and electric grids were coming together so that towns and agricultural communities could develop.

Palestine, the land of Zion, the original Jewish homeland. Strength in adversity suffused the religion, its holidays, its call to compassionate remembrance. Fervent belief that it was their destiny to return one day had brought religious Jews into the movement. Pragmatic leaders like Jakob, though daunted by the stark reality of inhospitable desert land, felt the evidence of their faith in the ancient monuments of Zion. Jakob visited the holy sites, the storied towns, the sources of Judaism's earliest civilizations: The Temple Mount where King Solomon built the great temple that Babylonians destroyed, and Jews rebuilt, and Romans left in ruins. The Wailing Wall for mourning century upon century of loss. Jakob mixed pilgrimage with meetings to encourage the rebuilders. Some of his colleagues were leading infrastructure and development projects. Some of the Galician youths he had inspired and funded were leaders in kibbutzim. They were the ones to carry it forward with a young person's energy now.

A few months before his journey in January of 1933, Adolf Hitler had been named chancellor in Germany representing only about a third of the electorate in a coalition government. Paramilitary Storm Troopers (Brownshirts) were roughing up Jews and communists in the land of Beethoven and Bach, Goethe and Schiller. How long could Germans accept a violent leader who manipulated the law, distorting civilized and democratic norms to get his way? Assimilated Jews in Vienna and Berlin doubted Germans would put up with it. A Zionist woman in Berlin named Recha Freier was not so sure. She started an organization called Youth Aliyah to resettle women and children in the homeland at a time when few thought well-educated German Jews would ever need sanctuary in Palestine.

Jakob went through the motions of applying for Palestinian visas for his family with mixed feelings. By Viennese cultural standards, Palestine was not civilized. His goal was to make a homeland for the persecuted, not for himself, and he never intended to loosen his patriotic feelings for Austria by leaving. Palestine needed farmers more than it needed lawyers. What kind of education could Paul get there, and how could Irma be happy in a desert? His work for Jews in Vienna was far from done. Jakob was the man in lederhosen and a Tyrolean hat with Paul and Irma in Austrian folk attire on the slopes of the Rax. He wanted more time spotting gentian violets poking through snow; hearing crampons crunch into glacier; breathing in thin, exhilarating air in view of dazzling Alpine peaks. His personal homeland was Austria. The visas stayed locked in a drawer.

Irma in Austrian folk dress with Jakob and Paul, mid-1930s

The Better German State

1934–1938

Jagged white peaks glistened over the green Tyrolean hamlet of Hinterbichl in late June 1936, when Irma and Paul, now thirteen, set out from their rustic half-timbered inn. Wispy clouds rode the thin Alpine air, famed for purifying the clear as bell voices of the Vienna Boys' Choir at their favorite retreat. Paul could no longer imitate their sound reliably. He had celebrated his bar mitzvah a month earlier in May, and his adolescent voice ricocheted like a bow loose on violin strings. With the school year complete and Jakob busy with work, mother and son took time to hike the glorious snow-patched slopes. They named the bright wildflowers that freckled the wet lower meadows as they went: purple primula, healing arnica, pincushions of pinks.

Irma wanted Paul to study in England when he was older. She had started teaching him English at home, and together they had been laughing their way through the tales of *Doctor Dolittle*, who spoke in animal talk to creatures like the bidirectional Pushmi-Pullyu. Though his parents would have liked him to study law like his father, he preferred the magic of chemistry, with its power to create and cure. The Ehrlichs often met like-minded people in Austrian mountain resorts. The previous summer at the posh

Madrisa Hotel in the Alps near the Swiss border at Gargellen, they had enjoyed the company of a professor of chemistry from England named Ralph Levy. He said he would welcome Paul if he came to study in England, so Irma kept in touch by letter.

....

Irma and Paul wandered off-trail at rocky outcrops to check over the edges for edelweiss, the wooly white star-shaped symbol of pristine Alpine hardiness. They kept track of their location by compass and horizon, always watchful for weather changes. Irma wore her traditional dirndl dress, folk costume of the Alpine peoples, handmade to her order in one of the local towns with ribbons of embroidered edelweiss flowers over a bright ensemble of cornflower blue and crimson. Paul wore the equally traditional lederhosen with suspenders and a Tyrolean felt hat. Irma, a look-alike for the fair-haired Swiss-German mountain girl Heidi, and her long-legged son were a welcome sight to a tall blond hiker who approached them from a distance. Irma recalled their encounter:

> We were hiking in the mountains and ran into the young Dutchman, [Leo] Knook, who had lost his way. He also was a guest at the inn. On the way down the mountain he was enthusiastic about Hitler Youth. On arrival at the hotel I told him we were Jewish and he could forget about us.
>
> When we came to the dining room that evening there was a bunch of red roses on the table, and the waitress came to tell me that the gentleman who had sent the flowers asked for the favor of being seated with us. When he left after a few days he sent greetings from Holland, and we kept up our correspondence ever since.

Clearly Knook hadn't seen Irma as Jewish or he might have weighed his words differently. Perhaps he was fooled by the edelweiss in her dress, an Alpine regional folkloric symbol under hijack by ultra-nationalistic Germans—though she wore the edelweiss in its original sense as a symbol of hardy resistance. Perhaps Knook was misguided by Hitler's crafty propaganda, or possibly he was the kind of person who would do her harm. Knook's conversation on the mountain had been charming and literary otherwise—he was a book publisher—and she had not let on while she was guiding him down the mountain that he was offending her. With the appearance of the roses and courtly apology at the table, Irma chose to educate Knook on the terrible price of Hitler's popularity and won a young admirer for life.

Unemployment had been near 30 percent when the National Socialists came to power in Germany in 1933, but by 1936 the economy under Hitler was rebounding. Munitions factories helped to put people back to work. Top-down economic measures forced German businesses to become public-private enterprises that contributed to national coffers. Social welfare helped the poorest. Social clubs filled young minds with nationalist fervor and taught them that anyone who did not conform was an enemy. Schoolbooks depicted Jews as vile, impure, greedy, ugly conspirators. Knook was one of many who failed to see that mistreatment of Jews signaled danger far beyond German borders.

On the first night dining with Knook at the inn at Hinterbichl, Irma explained why Jakob remained in Vienna and did not come to the mountains he loved: by speaking out for the Jewish people, he was saving Austria. Knook joined them at dinner each night after that until his return to the flatlands in Holland. One day he would come to her rescue, as she'd rescued him from the mountainside *and* his fog of illusion about Hitler.

....

By 1936 many had fallen in step with Hitler and his philosophies. Wild conspiracy theories, propaganda, and media control work better than we like to think. Organized violence by avid young enforcers like Brownshirts or Schutzstaffel (SS) men is more terrifying and effective in silencing dissent than we imagine. Former British prime minister Lloyd George visited Germany in 1936, thinking he would be able to judge true conditions in Germany by himself. He wrote about the Hitler phenomenon in the *Daily Express*:

> Whatever one may think of his methods, and they are certainly not those of a parliamentary country, there can be no doubt that he has achieved a marvelous transformation in the spirit of the people, in their attitude towards each other, and in their social and economic outlook.
>
> It is not the Germany of the first decade that followed the war—broken, dejected, and bowed down with a sense of apprehension and impotence. It is now full of hope and confidence, and a renewed sense of determination.
>
> As to his popularity, especially among the youth of Germany, there can be no manner of doubt. The old trust him; the young idolize him. It is not the admiration accorded to a popular Leader. It is the worship of a national hero who has saved his country from utter despondency and degradation.
>
> This great people will work better, sacrifice more, and, if necessary, fight with greater resolution because Hitler asks them to do so.
>
> Every well-wisher of Germany—and I count myself among them—earnestly pray that Goebbels's ranting speeches will not provoke another anti-Jewish manifestation. *Daily Express,* September 17, 1936

Lloyd George believed that Hitler deserved credit for saving Germany from communism and was not a military threat. But he ought to have known better. Already Hitler had stopped paying war reparations, taken back the Saarland, remilitarized the Rhineland in violation of signed treaties, boycotted Jewish businesses, dismissed Jewish civil servants, restricted Jewish access to schools, forbidden mixed marriages, and trumpeted his intention to annex Austria. Work camps were growing to contain political opponents, Gypsies, Jehovah's Witnesses, gays, and uncooperative Jews. England and surrounding European countries recovering from the Great War and the Great Depression hoped Hitler was only a nationalist, not a conqueror. They called for a boycott on German goods but did not intervene forcefully. Millions of Europeans thought Hitler too extreme to last.

....

Austrians felt the proximity of Nazism intensely. Austria had a tenth of Germany's population, 6.7 million to Germany's 67 million. It shared a five-hundred-mile border, a common language, and strong cultural affinity. Only religion divided them—mostly Protestants in northern Germany, Catholics in Austria—but the Christian bond was strong. A good percentage of Austrians saw Germany's remarkable economic turnaround and the apparent joy of their ethnic brethren and wanted to join them. They admired the way Hitler flouted international norms and restrictions—including the postwar ban on German unification with Austria.

Austria's government had been elected on a pro-independence ticket, but it was struggling with clashes between "Red Vienna" socialists, Catholic conservatives, and ethnic nationalists—the same toxic mix that had eased Hitler into power in Germany. In 1933 Austria's chancellor Engelbert Dollfuss suspended elections, recreated the municipal council and parliament with appointees, and banned all political parties including socialists and Nazis. But National Socialism flowed easily between borders until ten Austrian Nazis assassinated Chancellor Dollfuss in 1934 in a failed coup. The successor to the "Austro-fascist" Dollfuss was

Chancellor Kurt Schuschnigg, who imprisoned the perpetrators and called on Austrians to reject Hitler's vision for Germany, to stay pure and strong like the edelweiss, and to uphold Christian virtues in a way Germany did not. Austria, he said, should see herself as "the *better* German state."

....

A few Jews left Austria in the mid-1930s, but departures were mostly limited to those with excellent job prospects overseas, a family happy to receive them elsewhere, or very nervous dispositions. The outflow was hardly noticeable. Most stood their ground because their homes, livelihoods, and children and elderly parents were there and they all deserved to stay.

The "better German state" appointed Jakob Ehrlich to the Vienna Municipal Council in the same position he had won in the past election. His former law partner and head of the Jewish Community Organization, Desider Friedmann, was appointed to the national parliament. Jakob and Friedmann met regularly with Chancellor Schuschnigg to strategize on how to run the young country. The Nazi party remained banned. When Chancellor Schuschnigg needed an envoy to persuade European countries to support Austria's new currency, he sent Friedmann to London and got the needed endorsement.

Schuschnigg led an effort to return to democracy with a new national constitution in keeping with an independent Austria. Jakob spoke for the Jews when he told the municipal assembly in 1934 that "No one wants to deny the German and Christian character of the Austrian state." He affirmed that the Jewish minority would accept a new constitution based on Christian concepts, not racial ones. Jews were part of a Judeo-Christian civilization. They wanted civic equality and respect for Jewish cultural life, he said.

Jakob's position made him the sole voice for Vienna's 180,000 Jews and a minority of one on the forty-person council, and so he spoke passionately for the rights of his people. As 10 percent of Vienna, he said, the Jewish community deserved 10 percent of community-designated funds. Each January Jakob had the floor during budget deliberations. Jakob appealed to the Christian conscience of his Austrian colleagues with a significant fact: Jews held less than 1 percent of Vienna's government jobs but comprised 10 percent of the city's population. All would be better off with living up to common values of fairness, decency, and tolerance, he said, which would mean confronting workplace discrimination.

In 1935, Nazi Germany passed the Nuremberg Laws, which made Jews non-citizens and forbade Jews to employ young Gentile servants or marry Gentiles. This emboldened covert Nazis in Vienna. Catholic clergymen proposed to undermine Jews by boycotting Jewish stores before the Christmas holiday in 1937. Ultra-Germans including the city's Mayor Schmitz endorsed the idea. Jakob spoke forcefully against it at City Hall, and no such rule was made.

As pressures on Jakob grew, Irma joined by his side in the Wipplinger Street office to work as a legal secretary and relieve as much of his burden as she could. Typing his speeches and correspondence, she absorbed the motivational language of the Zionist movement. When she acted independently, she loved to win Jakob's appreciation: *"Das hast du gut gemacht"* ("Well done"). She received a note from her Protestant friend Marie von Kohoutek in Germany asking that she stop writing letters due to the hostile climate. Irma considered whether this was a betrayal, prudence, or both at once. By then, Irma had looked back at all the other eager German nationalists she had known in her youth—Professor Krogner, her high school literature teacher; the father of her classmate Maus Westen, who "kept strictly aloof" from Jewish students; the raucous German fraternities in Prague before National Socialism—and reassessed them as proto-Nazis in wait. Could they believe Hitler that Jews comprised a vast international conspiracy to get all the money and enslave them? Or did they feed on the fiction that Germans ought to purify Europe's gene pool before their glorious Aryan superrace was swamped by others? Vilification of an imaginary enemy is a well-worn tactic for inciting violence. Then, as now, ethno-nationalistic bonds of brotherhood found their narratives, symbols, and momentum.

Jakob, Friedmann, and others had long led the Jewish Community Organization without compensation. But community resources came under strain as doctors, lawyers, and professors who had lost their jobs in Germany spilled into Vienna seeking help. Jakob and his colleagues agreed that they needed to pay a full-time administrative director to do the job they had been doing as volunteers. They hired a younger man, Josef Löwenherz, to work under the board of directors.

Jakob continued to raise funds for the homeland in Palestine. Vienna's Jewish community honored Jakob once again in 1936, when at age fifty-nine, his name was inscribed in the golden book of the Keren Kajemet land fund for Palestine—a second recognition after the one received for the Keren Hayesod infrastructure fund in 1929. Palestine was taking in an average of forty thousand Jews annually between 1933 and 1936—many times the numbers of earlier years—as Jews from Germany began to flee. Austria's Jewish Community Organization helped the German Jews who came over their border to emigrate via Vienna. In 1937, however, mandate officials in Palestine lowered immigration quotas to quell open revolt by Arabs against British colonial rule. British authorities sought a compromise, but the revolt resumed.

Jakob reached the age of sixty a hero to Vienna's Zionists, with a reputation for compassionate and tireless dedication to Jewish equality. He began to think of retirement. Service on the Vienna Municipal Council was paid, he received a stipend for heading up the Austrian Zionist federation, and he had a few investments, including land in Brno (Brünn), Czechoslovakia. But he had neglected his private law practice in response to community demands. Soon his son, Paul, fourteen, would need funds for university, preferably abroad. Late in 1937, and much to his relief, Jakob landed a multiyear contract as legal counsel for Anker Insurance. Now he could step back from public service and let younger men carry on.

....

"What is the Jew Ehrlich doing on Vienna's German Council?" screamed the headline over an ugly distorted picture of Jakob Ehrlich's face on the cover of *Der Stürmer*, the hysterically anti-Semitic tabloid read by underground Nazis. Hitler had been threatening Austria's economy and independence openly. Jakob had used his allotted time during the municipal council's annual budget talks in January 1938 to defend equality of Jewish rights so eloquently that the speech was reported abroad. Jews at the next meeting of the Jewish Community Organization responded with a unanimous vote of commendation for Jakob's speech. But Jews seldom vote unanimously for anything. The few who still thought Jakob's speech was a show of bravado rather than bravery excused themselves from the room before the vote.

Hitler imposed one of his many impossible ultimatums. He promised *not to invade* Austria *if* Chancellor Schuschnigg added hand-selected covert Austrian Nazis to his cabinet—an infiltration certain to lead to a takeover. Schuschnigg was stuck. The last thing he wanted was to see Germans killing Germans on his watch. He addressed those in the public who stood by him:

> There is no question of ever accepting Nazi representatives in the Austrian cabinet. An absolute abyss separates Austria from Nazism. . . . We reject uniformity and centralization. . . . Christendom is anchored in our very soil, and we know but one God: and that is not the State, or the Nation, or that elusive thing, Race.
> —*Morning Telegraph*, January 5, 1938

How many Austrians wanted unification with Germany? How many wanted a better German state in Austria? Regardless of the answer, Austria was clearly the *weaker* German state. Schuschnigg saw that the tiny Austrian army was no match for the powerfully armed Germany, the Germany that rearmed in defiance of the League of Nations without consequences, the Germany that Britain's Lloyd George had deemed nonaggressive.

People now speak of "rising anti-Semitism" in 1920s and 1930s Europe as though it were a visible force with a discernible direction at the time. This is a view foreshortened by hindsight. Some were confused by social Darwinism, which posited survival of the fittest in a battle of race on race. Like Irma's friend Knook, what many saw was rising German nationalism and a will for self-determination that disguised systemic racism.

In March of 1938, a desperate Chancellor Schuschnigg announced a yes-or-no referendum on German unification to show the world what Hitler was doing and stop it. In a country that had not held a popular vote in years, Schuschnigg calculated that the "no's" would win by a slender margin if Hitler Youth–aged people (under twenty-four) did not qualify to vote. He scheduled the referendum for March 13, 1938.

But the world would never find out how many "better Germans" remained in Austria. Hitler took the proposed referendum as his signal to attack. A helpless Schuschnigg resigned on March 11, 1938. German soldiers entered Austria ready to fight but rested their arms when Austrian throngs came out to welcome them. Nazi insignia came out of closets and into the streets. Hitler was thrilled. On March 15, Hitler's open car drove through flowers and cheers to his new Vienna headquarters, the requisitioned Hotel Metropole, eleven minutes' walk from Café Central.

Hitler appointees took their seats in the vacated chairs of Austrian officials and replaced the old laws with their own. The *Lügenpresse* Hitler detested—the "lying press" or "fake news" in the parlance of a recent American president—was silenced. A restated referendum in April returned a miraculous 99.7 percent in favor of the annexation. Bravely, Paul's Czech nanny, Rosa Mazura, voted *nein*, no. Loyal Nazis counted the vote as they pleased. Years of resistance melted away in a flash. The Ehrlich family heard the songs of triumphant German troops marching past their apartment.

Rosa and Sylvester Mazura, Nazi resisters

Shock Waves

March 1938

———◆———————◆———

Come with me into Jakob and Irma's world in March of 1938. Set aside your cache of foreknowledge about a time we call World War II. Unlearn the terms "Holocaust" and "mass deportation," because no one at the time could conceive of such things. People knew that Hitler would attempt to remake Austria in Germany's image, but they had no idea how quickly aggressions would escalate.

The annexation unfolded methodically, with officials concentrating at first on taking over the reins of government. Newswire images of Hitler's hero's welcome into Vienna and his questionable referendum helped to prevent war-weary neighboring countries from intervening. Austrians appeared to be getting what they said they wanted after World War I: an all-German country. Jews and other Nazi political targets knew they were in for hell, but what sort of hell, they had no way of predicting.

Jakob was a highly visible political opponent and a Jew. He had a target pinned on his chest. Irma, forty-seven, had a son set to go abroad for study soon. She had thrived on pride in Jakob's outspoken valor and public recognition as a statesman, and she aided in his success. Now her fortitude would be tested. Irma and Jakob had only ten more days together.

Irma told me this story in a three-hour sitting in the shady backyard of my family's home, in the summer of 1973 after my first year of college. At eighty-three, she sat straight-backed in a chair with her legs in a ladylike cross. Her stately head was rimmed by a brush of white hair, and she looked battle-worn and proud, like an old lion. She had waited to tell me this part of her life, she said, until I was old enough to process it without being scarred. Irma's story of March through September 1938 seemed to have no natural place to pause. The words spilled like a flood when they came, and I saw that the retelling forced her to relive it. It was clear that every detail had a role in the outcome. She described it almost exactly as she wrote it down later:

I

I cannot leave, March 11–15, 1938
Friday, March 11 [when Chancellor Schuschnigg resigned] started normally. We had breakfast at seven a.m., after I had served Jakob his orange juice in bed. Paul went to school and I went shopping, then to the tram, and I was in his office at nine. Jakob took his time, read the paper, and arrived later. In the afternoon Paul had a violin lesson with Ernst Rosenberg at four p.m. at home. Jakob arrived home between four and five p.m. with the shattering news that the Germans were invading. It was paralyzing.

After Ernst left, I leaned against the big bookcase in the living room, face-to-face with Jakob, and said with determination, "Take your suitcase and go to my parents in Prague immediately," to which he replied, "I cannot leave. I represent the Jewish people, and you and Paul would be hostages," to which I replied, "You won't be able to do anything for them here. Go. They won't do anything to us." Instead, Jakob phoned Löwenherz [director of Vienna's Jewish Community Organization] and they decided he should come over after dinner to discuss steps to take for the community. It was a very quiet dinner, each of us with our own fears.

Jakob left after dinner and returned very late. I was in bed terror-stricken, and relieved when I finally heard his key opening the door. He took a pill and immediately fell asleep. That night I did not sleep at all. I heard the noise from the meeting place of the young Nazis—the former soup kitchen—their triumphant songs, their marching steps. For a few minutes, just when the sky began to brighten, I dozed off. In my dream I saw two SS men, dressed in black uniforms with the insignia of skull and crossbones on their caps—I had never seen an SS man before—enter by the window, lift Jakob, and disappear with him through the window. I woke up in horror. Jakob was sleeping peacefully next to me.

That same night Bernhard Altmann left. [Altmann, a friend and textile magnate, slipped across the border to get to France. His quick thinking saved his family and led ultimately to their recovery of the Gustav Klimt masterpiece *Woman in Gold*.] Other people we knew tried to leave the country via Brno, Czechoslovakia. When the train was stopped at the Czech border, some managed to run across while others were caught and brutally put back on trains to Vienna. Many houses of wealthy Jewish families were ransacked by gangs of Nazis. The chauffeur and maids of our friends Otto and Agathe Krassny doped Puck, their giant schnauzer, bound the Krassnys to chairs, and made them open their safe. The servants took the jewelry and everything else in the safe, and drove away in the Krassnys' car.

Stories of ominous happenings spread amongst the Jewish population. Men and women, irrespective of age, given away by janitors, cooks, or maids, had to scrub the streets. Old Orthodox Jews were caught in the second district, paraded in the Prater, molested and beaten, their long hair and side locks shorn. All of that started the moment the first troops entered Vienna.

On Saturday morning, we were unsure of what was happening around us. We did not go to the office as usual. Jakob went to meet friends to discuss the situation. I visited with Nellie Altmann at the hospital where she had been operated upon, taking along the beautiful azalea I had received from recent guests. She was unaware of her husband's departure [Bernhard Altmann saved her from abroad]. We strolled, foreboding in our hearts, silent, terror-stricken. Above us roared the first German planes, diving low and showering the street with pamphlets announcing the next step by showing the map of Czechoslovakia between the open jaws of the German beast.

Before leaving the apartment that afternoon I had a sudden idea. I cleared all the silverware from the drawers in the lovely Biedermeier chest that harbored all our fine china, glasses, and relics, and took it to [Irma's helpmate and Paul's nanny] Rosa's husband, Sylvester, on the ground floor of the house. I thought our passports were in one of the drawers I emptied.

When Jakob and I arrived back home, Rosa broke the shattering news that the Gestapo had searched the apartment in our absence and confiscated the passports [in a coordinated raid that included Sigmund Freud's house]. It was the first frightening omen. While I am writing this it suddenly occurs to me that Jakob should have left the house immediately, spent the night somewhere else, and left the country [Irma was still trying to bargain with fate as she wrote this, forgetting that he refused to go]. If lucky, he might have reached Switzerland. It was possible to get there without a passport up until March 31. It was hazardous from the beginning to get into Czechoslovakia, where my parents were.

These were days of an indescribable, agonizing suspense. Jakob had premonitions from the start. The proud man wanted me to ask an ardent young Nazi who lived with his parents in the apartment below ours to intervene on his behalf, so that if arrested he would not be beaten. He worried for himself, Paul, me, the Viennese Jewry. I was defiant, outraged that all the Nazi scum, anybody with high boots and a swastika, could do anything he wanted with me, that I had no rights whatsoever. If I was not wanted, I wanted to leave as fast as possible.

Sunday morning, March 13 [the day of Hitler's referendum], we went to the office. Neither Immerglück [Jakob's schoolmate, now law partner] nor his secretary was there. We burned all of Jakob's collected speeches, clippings from papers reporting on his activities and public appearances, his publications, Zionist literature referring to him, his remarks as president of the Zionist Congress held in Vienna in July 1925, and his famous speeches as counselor to the City of Vienna, with the exception of the last one, which was still at home.

Sunday afternoon we were with wealthy friends who had family in London. I suggested we leave immediately for London, rent or buy a house with their help, and take care of children for people who wanted to get them out of Austria. Jakob's name would be a recommendation and I, speaking English and being an experienced teacher, would be able to manage the enterprise [another woman did just that, as recounted by Mona Golabek and Lee Cohen in *The Children of Willesden Lane*]. In the few days which still remained, nothing was done.

The first thing Jakob insisted I do was to write to my uncle Siegmund Singer in Anadarko, Oklahoma, and ask for an affidavit, stressing the urgency of his immediate compliance. [The US required that a guarantor promise support in case of need in America.] Another letter was to go to Ralph Levy, the professor of chemistry we met in the Alps in 1933, with whom we had discussed the possibility of Paul's study in England after he graduated from the academic high school. Jakob insisted that I ask the Levys for the favor of taking care of Paul until we could get there, which he hoped would be by summer. We asked that in the meantime, they enroll Paul in a school of their choice.

It is hard to revive the feelings and agonies of the next weeks. I was in complete shock. There was a certain protective numbness, which made it possible for me to function reasonably well, and also an outrage. Suddenly you have been transformed from a respected citizen into a non-person. Dangers were all around. People were picked up in the streets and disappeared. Nobody knew what was going on and what would happen next. Any moment anything could happen. I thought the world would not allow it. That Roosevelt would stop it. There were ominous knocks on doors in the dark hours. Prominent people, mostly Jews, but also Marxists and noted Catholics were arrested. I heard of friends, political allies, who disappeared. Who would be next?

....

Hitler's well-briefed military men removed all potential opponents, took over the media, and installed their own party-driven bureaucracy. Nazis raided the office of the Jewish Community Organization in order to use the records against Jews—as foreseen by Irma and Jakob in their frantic burning of Jakob's political files.

Methods for forcing Jewish emigration that had been refined in Germany over a five-year span went into effect immediately in Austria. Jews holding government jobs were dismissed. Nazis preserved a facade of legality as they forced owners of companies to sign their holdings over to the Reich and redistributed them to Christian bosses who obeyed orders. Schools had to follow the Nazi curriculum glorifying the "Aryan" race and depicting Jews as vile parasites and worse.

Irma still thought that Jakob's reputation would protect them, and she looked for respect and human decency in a quickly degrading environment. She continued her written account:

2

Don't let him starve, March–April 1938
Nazi government orders came fast and thick. In Germany conditions had deteriorated slowly, step by step, and never with the brutal recklessness as in Austria. And the *gemütliche* (comfy or smug) Viennese enjoyed themselves immensely. Everything had been painstakingly prepared in secret. You did not know who your friends were. Dr. Smitka, earlier Jakob's legal assistant and friend, wore a swastika hidden under his lapel. A Zionist lawyer friend's office partner was Arthur Seyss-Inquart [one of Hitler's handpicked Austrian Nazis for the government takeover], who would become

the Nazi governor of the Netherlands. When I opened the mail on one of the following days, I found a case had been decided negatively on the grounds that the attorney who represented it was a Jew. Non-Jews had to wear a swastika under the threat of heavy penalty for failing to do so. Many who looked Jewish were snatched in the street and arrested. Jews were not allowed to sit on benches in parks and public places. Stores were marked as Jewish and Nazis took them over. Aryan maids had to leave their Jewish employers. Automobiles of Jewish owners were confiscated.

Parents made frantic efforts to get their children out of the country. There were whispered reports that Youth Aliyah scouts led groups of youngsters over mountains and by devious routes to southern ports and Palestine. For high pay a woman smuggled children into Bohemia by wading with them across a river at the border in the midst of the night.

We went to the office together each morning. We returned for lunch, often walking, German planes roaring overhead, German armored cars in the streets, tanks with grinning German soldiers, SS men strutting around. We scarcely spoke, both of us in deep thought. Jakob did not return to the office in the afternoons. Some lawyers who lived in the neighborhood came to ask for advice. I resented it, because they robbed the haunted man of the precious time still left to him. Wilma Kohn, the youngest daughter of Dr. Kohn of Budweis, whose legal assistant Jakob had been for four years, and who had married a non-Jewish officer stationed in Budweis during World War I, came to discuss the possibility of a sham divorce [to protect him]. I remember that this call was on Thursday afternoon, March 17.

Later, we walked over to the Schwoners' for dinner.
Dr. Benno Schwoner was director of Anker, an important insurance agency with main offices in Zurich. Jakob,
Dr. Schwoner, and Dr. Immerglück had been classmates
in high school. A few months earlier, Dr. Schwoner had
arranged for Jakob to be the attorney for some of Anker's accounts, which secured a nice steady income. And
one or two weeks before the Anschluss [annexation by
the Germans], Jakob had been named director of the
new Vienna office of the Keren Hayesod [the Jerusalem
building fund]. Jakob had said to me happily that from
now on income from these two clients would make him
independent of any others, and so make our lives pleasant
and carefree.

Jakob thought Schwoner might have valuable information because of his international connections. But
there was only a fine meal, general talk, fears, and apprehensions. The next day, we heard that the Schwoners had
left for Switzerland with some Swiss officials who had
come to secure their smooth departure. Their apartment
was sealed and later everything was confiscated. Not to
arouse suspicion, everything had been left in place. The
evening before we had admired the central heating they
had had installed, and a refrigerator, which no one else
in Vienna had.

Dinner at the Schwoners' had been on Thursday,
March 17. Friday and Saturday morning we were at the
office. Dr. Immerglück had a new Jewish secretary. Her
little girl was in the hospital sick with diphtheria and was
refused serum [as a Jew; the child recovered].

On Sunday, March 20, we were at home. Tony, the
maid, had left and I was fully dressed. Jakob was still in
the bathroom when the bell rang. Two young Vienna

Police lads had come for him. We had no chance to talk. They sat on the red chairs in the foyer and waited for him. I brought him his clothes. In leaving he said, "*Lass ihn nicht hungern*" ["Don't let him starve," a phrase Jakob often used in jest to mean "Take good care of him"]. The door closed. I saw that he had left behind a handkerchief and rushed after him. I caught up with them in the middle of the stairs. He turned around to take the handkerchief, but his gaze was already fixed far away. I don't think he saw me.

This was one of the longest days of my life. I was in shock and completely paralyzed. I do not remember how long I sat on the red chair in the foyer, when the telephone rang. It was Mr. Gutman [a friend], who wanted to talk to Jakob. When he heard what had happened he came immediately and insisted I spend the day at his house. He would try to find out where Jakob had been taken. Mr. Gutman found out that Jakob was in a Vienna prison. [Nazis put Jakob in a cell with the anti-Semitic Mayor Schmitz at Rossauerlaende Prison to undermine both men.] I had to break the news to Paul when he came home—a heartbreaking task. All night I tried to figure out what to do.

The following days were full of anxiety and uncertainty. Dr. Desider Friedmann, former Jewish representative to parliament; Engineer Robert Stricker, head of the "Revisionist" [right-wing] Zionist faction; leaders of all Zionist factions; leaders of all B'nai B'rith groups; wealthy industrialists; and businessmen began to crowd Vienna prisons.

I phoned my sister Edna Werner in Prague to ask her to call the wives of Hans Kreindl and Dr. von Schreitter [prison mates of her husband in Siberia]. I had met them in a coffee house once in Prague. Edna had been friends with their wives ever since she got a letter from her husband, Fritz, after six years in Siberia with the news that he, Kreindl, and Schreitter were alive. Both men were Sudeten Germans with connections in the highest National Socialist circles. The wives promised their husbands' help [in the belief that a word from the right person might free Jakob].

I went to the office every morning. Afternoons belonged to Paul, as before. There were new arrests every day, horror stories, rumors. On the streetcar, I was sometimes startled by the brilliance of diamond earrings worn by lower-class women. Others wore rings with precious stones. The Viennese mob had lots of fun. Returning from the office one noon, past the beltway before the church at the upper Wäringerstrasse, I saw laughing, jeering crowds shouting obscenities.

One day, it was announced that wives were allowed to visit prisoners at certain hours in the afternoon. One was allowed to bring items of clothes and food. Long before the allotted time, there was already a line of waiting women in front of the prison. Slowly, to my despair, we inched our way ahead. I had been so excited, so full of expectations. Finally, I reached the gate. It opened to a dimly lit corridor. Before me were a couple of women, the first facing the first of the prisoners. The third or fourth was Jakob. I saw him in his striped prison garb. At that moment a voice announced the end of the visits. Jakob had seen me and waved his hand. There was excitement, a shuffle. Rude guards pushed us out. I walked the long way home, crying, trying to control myself before facing Paul at home.

....

By the time they entered Vienna, Nazis had compiled a list of 150 opposition figures and invented reasons for arrests. Jakob Ehrlich and other leaders of the Jewish community were on that handwritten list. An imaginary charge about Jakob collecting arms for resistance went on file in a Nazi drawer to cover up their lawless intent. When the city prison began to overflow, Nazis made a show of crowding the once-dignified former leaders of Vienna into open trucks to convey them in a humiliating way to a more distant prison. This warning to the public was the infamous *Prominententransport*, the transport of the prominent. At first, a promise to sign away assets and emigrate at once might lead to a Jewish prisoner's freedom.

I recall the stricken look on my father Paul's face when he pointed out a picture on page 290 of a book published by the Historical Museum of Vienna in 1988 called *Wien 1938* and said, "My father is second from the left, nearly covered up by a third person. Löwenherz is the person at the extreme right." He had never seen the image before. Postcards written to Irma and Paul from Jakob in prison said, "I'm healthy and doing fine," and "How is Paul?" next to the rules for prisoner notes that took up half of the card. Irma resumes:

3

Pray it doesn't last long, April–June 1938

There was nobody to advise me, everybody full of fear for their own person, everything so unprecedented. During an agonized night, I naively decided to get in touch with the Gestapo to try to convince them of Jakob's integrity, high moral standards, and patriotism. I took his medals for distinction in World War I to Gestapo headquarters. There was a line. I had to wait. When my turn finally came, I found myself opposite a man with a stony face, uninterested, scarcely looking at me. The interview was short. He let me talk a while, grabbed the medal and looked at the front page of an open big journal on his desk. "*Ihr Mann ist heute Nacht nach Dachau verschickt worden.*" ("Your husband is being sent to Dachau tonight.") I was dismissed. It was a terrible shock.

Still, I did not know what "Dachau" meant [it was a brutal work camp across the border in Germany—the first German concentration camp—but no one knew what else it would become within a few years]. On April 1, 1938, the first transport left for Dachau with members of the government including Mayor Schmitz and other prominent politicians and notable people. I do not know how I got home or what happened next. I only remember that I wondered that the sun could be shining and that there was such an unusually beautiful spring.

I continued to go to the office. On one of the following days, getting off the tram and crossing the Ring, I came face-to-face with Dr. Glaser, one of the directors of the Landesbank and a close friend of Dr. Schwoner. He asked how Jakob was. When I told him that he had been deported to Dachau, his face fell and he said with a faltering voice: "*Beten Sie für Ihn dass es nicht lang macht!*" ("Pray for him that it won't last long!") Then it dawned on me what he meant. I was in shock.

It was the end of April and time was running out. On April 29, Paul was expelled from the academic high school and assigned to one in the ninth district where Jewish boys from several other schools were assembled. Through the windows of the streetcar on my daily ride to the office I could see the windows of the stores smeared over and marked "Jews." Most of the larger stores were taken over by Nazi loyalists.

During the few days that Jakob was still at home he told me the names of people whose payment was due, in case he would be arrested. A certain Fleischmann to whom I had sent a note appeared promptly and threatened to denounce me to the Gestapo. A Jewish lawyer had no right to ask for payment. [The same man, claiming to be an old friend of Jakob, later asked for help from MP Barnett Janner in London and Rabbi Stephen Wise in New York.] The days dragged on. One day, Robert Stricker [Zionist leader], who had been on the *Prominententransport* with Jakob and later released, as was Löwenherz, told me Jakob would be home any moment. That was an agonizing, futile wait.

Prisoners at concentration camps were allowed to exchange letters with their families once a week—thirty words, I think. I was proud to report to Jakob that everything in the office was well taken care of and, in my last letter, that Uncle Sieg's affidavit [guarantee of backup support in America] had arrived. Jakob acknowledged this in his last letter. It was a great comfort to me that Jakob believed there would be a future for us.

In the office on a standing desk was the big record book with the dates of hearings and important data. When arriving at the office on May 16 I checked the page facing me as usual and saw to my horror that I had overlooked a most important date by a few days. A great amount of my parents' money was involved. Jakob administered my parents' money. For reasons of taxation and interest rates, their assets were booked in a special way that only he knew.

I was in a panic. Next morning, before office hours, I went to see the man concerned. It was a long ride. He lived in one of the farthest outskirts of Vienna. I found him in a dimly lit shed in a field. The small man listened attentively to my presentation, looking to the ground. Silence. My heart sank. What could I expect? Then: "*Haben Sie keine Angst. Ich werde Ihnen nichts antun.*" ("Have no fear. I won't do you any harm.") Under the shock of that time my memory of facts and figures is blurred. I do not recall the legal aspects of this episode; I know only that by my omission my parents could have lost their money. And how would I have stood before Jakob?

I cannot describe my relief. It was such a beautiful day, this May 17. I was so elated on the long ride to the office! I had scarcely settled at my desk when Dr. Smitka appeared for a visit with Dr. Immerglück. When he saw me he came over to my desk and asked for Jakob, not having heard of his deportation. Dr. Smitka was the illegitimate son of an archduke, and I assumed he had connections with the Nazis in high positions. I pleaded with him—that he had known Jakob's character, his high moral standards, etc., and I begged him to intervene on his behalf, which he promised to do.

A few minutes later the telephone rang. An uncultured voice said: "*Ihr Mann hat gestern einen Herzschlag gehabt. Er ist gestorben.*" ("Your husband had a heart attack yesterday. He is dead.")

The phone fell from my hand. I don't know what happened next. It must have been some time before Löwenherz arrived and took me home by taxi. Paul opened the door, happily waving a letter. "*Mutti, der Vati hat geschrieben.*" ("Mom, Dad has written.") The Gestapo had come to the house, so Rosa knew of Jakob's death but had refused to tell Paul.

....

Dr. Löwenherz took us to his house. I had no will to resist. I am oblivious to the next few hours. I only know Paul cried with pain till he fell asleep exhausted on my lap. Erna Patak was also there. In the late afternoon, Dr. Löwenherz took us to stay with friends, the Morgensterns. Paul and I spent the night together as once I had spent it with my mother who had come to me when Erwin had died on the battlefield.

We stayed with the Morgensterns one day? Two? Three? We left and someone took us home when Rosa phoned that my parents had arrived. Who had informed them? They may have read it in the paper. The news of Jakob's death went around the world. My parents had traveled through the night on trains full of Czech soldiers. There was mobilization in Czechoslovakia [against feared invasion by Hitler]. They had come with luggage and planned to stay with us during the first terrible weeks. Due to the ominous political situation and danger for their safety, friends insisted they return to Prague after the funeral.

Jakob's early death at Dachau caused a considerable furor in Vienna and also in the foreign press and Jewish papers abroad. Mention was prohibited in Viennese papers, but the news spread like wildfire. He was known for his noble character, integrity, and courage as a political figure. He was the first prominent Viennese to die at Dachau.

....

To everybody's amazement his coffin was sent for burial. (An urn was more common.) He was buried May 22 in an honorary grave. I don't remember how we got to the cemetery. I was told Eichmann [see next chapter] was there during the short ceremony. Leaving, I saw Adolf Böhm [author, Jewish historian, head of the Jewish National Fund for Palestine, and family friend close to Paul] standing by himself, sobbing. Long after the funeral people visited Jakob's grave as that of a martyr's to pray and leave small stones, an old Jewish custom. I was told it was covered with innumerable tokens from these visits.

During the following weeks many visitors came, I don't recall who. I remember that for a few days I lost my voice. I could not eat. Friends came with sandwiches from a famous delicatessen in the Dorotheer Alley and forcibly fed me. Ernst Rosenberg, the music teacher, came to comfort Paul. I stopped going to the office, was unable to plan anything during the following weeks until one day Paul said, "Everyone is leaving—when do we go?"

Jakob Ehrlich

Into the Eye of the Storm

June 1938

◆━━━━━◆

In 1955, Zionist and lawyer Leopold Friedmann dedicated the Jaakov (Hebrew for Jakob) Ehrlich Lodge in Tel Aviv, Israel, beginning with this memory:

> It was a cold and rainy morning, the 22nd of May in 1938, when a small group—mostly men—assembled in the mortuary of the Jewish sector of Vienna's Central Cemetery. Solemn, subdued, faces distorted with pain, there was no loud word to be heard, only restrained sobbing. Two days earlier a coffin had arrived from Dachau, returning to the Zionists and to all Jews the first of Vienna's precious dead—the body of Jakob Ehrlich. Like lightning, the news had spread by word of mouth to many hundreds who asked to attend the funeral, but they were turned away because the Gestapo forbade a public gathering. The coffin was opened to identify the body in a back room, and then brought forth to the hall. Only the traditional prayers for the dead were allowed. Any speech, any eulogy, was forbidden.

The eyes of those attending spoke eloquently of the pain and mourning, in sympathy with the lady in black, who stood with a half-grown youth, crying inwardly, beside the coffin. Distributed among the mourners were Gestapo spies watching with gloating and hate-filled eyes. Then the coffin went out to the grave accompanied by prayer songs. A few shovels full of earth were all the mourners could send into the grave with their friend and leader.

Standing in dripping rain that day in 1938 at Zentralfriedhof were two men locked in a command-and-control struggle over the lives of Vienna's Jews. Adolf Eichmann was the swaggering thirty-two-year-old SS man in charge of enforcing Jewish emigration. Josef Löwenherz, former director of the shuttered Jewish Community Organization, had been released from Dachau as a bound man, answerable to Eichmann. In her memoir, Irma remembered how Jakob supported Löwenherz:

Dr. Josef (Juzel, Juzek) Löwenherz was named office director of the Jewish Community, a paid job, only shortly before the Nazi takeover after a vicious struggle within the various factions of the community. This had caused Jakob great worries. Only Jakob's prestige, his influence as municipal councilor, and his desperate efforts prevented takeover of the organization by a "commissar" (loyal Nazi appointee) even before Hitler came. All the non-Zionist groups of the Jewish community engaged in a bitter struggle against the paid position. They denounced the Zionists for having "two fatherlands" and not being trustworthy Austrian patriots. Löwenherz was implored by his friends to step down in view of the dangerous political situation, but he stubbornly refused to do so. He won the position and it saved his life. He was released from Dachau after just a few days.

Löwenherz's release came at the cost of agreeing to expedite the Nazi policy of mass exodus of Austria's Jewish people. At Dachau, Eichmann had interviewed senior Zionists Jakob Ehrlich, Friedmann, and Stricker before Löwenherz. Only Löwenherz agreed to cooperate. We do not know the content of all interviews, but Irma said Jakob would never have collaborated. Once released, Löwenherz tried to get other Zionist leaders including Jakob released, but Eichmann had other plans. Nazis decommissioned the Jewish Community Organization and drove Löwenherz hard. They chose to work with the Zionist faction because of their connection with Palestine—the "second fatherland" non-Zionists had feared and now relied upon as a destination. In a letter to his superior in Berlin on May 8, 1938, Eichmann reported that the Zionist newspaper was his mouthpiece:

> *Tomorrow I will check again on the offices of the Jewish Community and the Zionists. I do that at least once every week. They are completely in my hands here; they dare not take a step without checking with me first.*
> —VIRTUAL JEWISH LIBRARY

Methods to induce "voluntary" emigration developed in Germany over five years went into effect immediately in Austria. Jews lost their livelihoods and faced hazards from both officials and self-appointed vigilantes on the streets. All prior Austrian passports were invalidated. Nazis set up processes to make sure they extracted all of the Jews' assets in the name of the Reich, no matter how long it took. Löwenherz had to guide the Jewish community through the harassment and legalistic obstacles. Jews needed a new passport issued by Ostmark, Germany's name for Austria under the Third Reich; a hard-to-obtain visa from a welcoming country; certification of assets so Nazis could appropriate what they wanted; and paperwork from a fiendish labyrinth of permits, fees, and taxes. Poor Jews needed aid with papers and travel finance. Eichmann fixed quotas for monthly emigration that Löwenherz had to meet.

When Irma emerged from her trance of mourning she had one driving purpose: to get Paul out. She could not understand why Eichmann was at her husband's funeral—and certainly not mourning. She thought her own life was over, she said later. It was a great comfort to her that Paul might go to England under the care of Ralph Levy, the chemistry professor at Cambridge.

Fourteen-year-old Paul had been so sheltered from fear of anti-Semitism that he recalled only one incident that could have gone badly. Riding his bicycle through an alley he passed a Nazi tough who growled, "Scram, or I'll have you scrubbing the streets." Irma navigated for him straight through her grief. She wrote:

I

On June 9, I left the house for the first time with the American affidavit to have it registered. I stood in line for a long time and got a receipt because in those days affidavits were often stolen and sold to Jews at the community center. People without receipts lost their position on the waiting list, which might mean catastrophe.

A few days later, my sister wrote me that my uncle Siegmund Singer in Anadarko, Oklahoma, wanted to withdraw his affidavit. On hearing of Jakob's death, he feared we would become his dependents. She and my mother had implored him not to withdraw it. I wrote him that I would not ask for any favors, but that it was Paul's life I had to save and that the affidavit was essential. I pledged never to ask him for a penny, and to support Paul myself.

At that time I thought only of getting Paul out of the country. The idea did not occur to me that I could leave at the same time [her mind in triage prioritized her son]. By talking to people I became aware of the ever more threatening situation and began to wind up our affairs.

I had legal advice from the lawyer Dr. Arthur Reik, but I was soon aware that I would have to act alone in all practical matters. Having relied so completely on Jakob, I had to learn how. I phoned Emil Krassny, Jakob's closest friend [from boyhood in Kroměříž], and he asked to see me. He had stopped going to the prestigious medical office he shared with Dr. Lanzer. When I got off the streetcar, he was waiting there with his wife, Erna, visibly agitated, and did not take me to their house. We walked the streets aimlessly for a while. It was clear he was scared to be compromised by me [someone was watching them]. I learned my lesson and went back home.

Lawyer Arthur Reik was a former member of Ivria, the Zionist student organization that Jakob had belonged to, and shared his law office with Leopold Friedmann [whose eulogy opens this chapter]. Jakob had held him in high regard professionally. He advised me on actions to take. One day, I was called by the Creditanstalt Bank to pick up Jakob's life insurance payment. To Dr. Reik's amazement, I was paid his life insurance while the Gestapo kept up the pretext that his death was caused by a heart attack. [Nazis were too legalistic not to follow the rules of payout for a "natural" death because prison murder of public officials was still taboo; they did not care about that later.] There was a scandal just before the annexation in March; the president of the company had committed suicide, and the insurance payments were reduced. Of the original 15,000 Austrian schillings, we received 10,000, which was still a considerable amount at the time. I returned home with a suitcase full of banknotes. I distributed them under our heavy oriental carpets and stuffed them into sofas. The process of settling Jakob's estate could begin. What I did not know was that this might have taken considerable time and, as in many tragic cases, might have prevented our departure [all pending matters had to be settled].

First, I had to make an appointment with a notary. Dr. Reik told me that the one I was assigned to in Währing was a Catholic and I needn't be afraid of him. He was pleasant and friendly. Paul and I were heirs, each due half of the total. He told me to write an inventory of all we had [Eichmann's circulars told all Jews they had to declare their assets between April 26 and June 30]. Dr. Reik also told me that I was under observation by of the Gestapo, and that Eichmann knew of my every step. I wrote the inventory in the privacy of the maid's room, which opened to the yard. The nights were hot, and I remember how pleasant it felt to write on the white marble table stored in that room.

When I returned to the notary he told me to take all the assembled material to the district judge of the 19th district, Hofrat Braun. The notary said Braun was a rabid Nazi, but I might impress him by talking [persuasively] as I had to him. He advised me to go alone, under no circumstances to send my lawyer. He suggested I offer him my half of the inheritance, as I would not be able to get it out of the country anyway, and keep Paul's share to pay for his education abroad. He wished me good luck, and I left with trepidation and fear of things to come.

I reported to Dr. Reik, who confirmed the notary's opinion of the official. Full of anxiety, I made my appointment and went to the court at Döbling. A secretary was sitting at his desk in the room I entered. "*Was wollen S'*?"("What do you want?") "I have an appointment with Herr Hofrat Braun." "For what purpose?" "Emigration." "*Wir wollen dass Ihr krepiert, nicht auswandert.*" ("We want you to perish, not emigrate.")

At that moment, the judge opened the door and waved me in. He was a foxy little man. I handed him my file. He looked at it for a while, then, not looking at me at all, was about to dismiss me. I gathered all my courage and started talking. He listened without moving or looking up. I offered him my share of Jakob's inheritance and asked him to let Paul keep his for education abroad. He said, "Your case has to be cleared by the Ministry of Finance. The summer recess begins Friday. Let your papers be picked up by your lawyer on Thursday." I was dismissed.

I went to Dr. Reik's office. He was waiting for me full of apprehension. He and Dr. Friedmann were jubilant when I told them my story. Thursday he went to the court to get our file. The secretary said, "Was wollen S'?" Dr. Reik replied, "Den Akt der Witwe des Dr. Jakob Ehrlich." ("The case of the widow of Jakob Ehrlich.") The secretary did not hand Dr. Reik the file but called to a woman who had just entered the room: "Was wollen Sie, verfluchte Judensau?" ("What do you want, you damned Jewish sow?") The woman started yelling back how dare he call her a Jewess, she was of pure Aryan blood. Startled by the screaming, the judge opened the door, saw Dr. Reik, and handed him our file. I was waiting in Dr. Reik's office. He was very excited when he returned and reported the scene at the court to me.

On Friday, he was to take the file for final approval to the Finance Ministry. I waited in his office. When Dr. Reik arrived at the Ministry foyer and asked for the official, he was told the vacation had already begun. Dr. Reik was standing there horror-stricken when he heard a voice. The official stood before him. He had left but forgotten something he needed in his desk drawer and returned to pick it up. "I wanted to take the Ehrlich case to the Ministry for its completion but saw to my consternation that it was already closed!" The official took the file, returned to his office, and after a short while came back with the approval of the case; the estate was settled. [Let's assume he got his payola.]

We owe our lives to this coincidence, as to many others. Normally, it took months for inheritance cases to be concluded. When cases dragged on, assets were seized and the Jewish owners were thrown into camps. That was a close shave.

2

I had been in mourning and had a lot of catching up to do. Ellie Friedmann, wife of representative Desider Friedmann, and Sofie Löwenherz, wife of Josef (Juzel, Juzek) Löwenherz, were of great help. Due to Juzek's position as office manager of the Jewish Community Organization and Sofie's as president of the Women's International Zionist Organization, their home was a center of information. People came to Sofie with their worries, asking for favors and help, and with tales, mostly of woe. People made frantic efforts to get their children out of the country.

By this time it was July. We were still hostages and needed new passports. When news of Jakob's death had reached Palestine, the provisional government cabled visas for us immediately. Friends advised me I should make sure that they were deposited at the British embassy, since it was known that a black market existed for these precious documents. I had an interview with Mr. Kendrick, the British ambassador, who assured me that he had the visas. He said he had followed Jakob's career and admired his courage and character.

When summer vacation began in July I tried to keep Paul busy, also to prepare him with some professional skills [photography lessons], should it be necessary for him to help earning money. At Sofie's, I heard of auditions for scholarships at the Jerusalem Conservatory with permits to enter the country. The man in charge was a fraud, and none of the kids, some of them really gifted, ever reached Jerusalem. Trusting him, they lost other chances and subsequently, their lives.

As the weeks of waiting passed, I had some moving experiences of people's concern for me. Emanuel Weissman appeared one day. He urgently pleaded with me to go with Paul to Australia. It was a new land of promise, he had relatives there, and he would take care of us. He was sure I would find work; life was inexpensive there. One day I had a letter from Sweden. There was a group there working for the families of political victims. I should let them know confidentially whether it was true that we needed help.

Dr. Leopold Ehrlich came one day, a cousin of Jakob's. He was a noted author [pen name Hichler]. His books are a manifestation of his love for the common Viennese people, their dialect, and their national traits. I think Jakob appreciated his cousin's nobility [in trusting folk who were proving untrustworthy], though they were diametrically opposed politically. Leopold made a generous offer of support, which I did not accept. I thanked him but said I would work for Paul and was sure to be able to succeed. I don't know why I was so sure, but then and in the following years, my pride was a help.

Rosa was with me one afternoon when a visitor arrived. In came a tall, handsome young man who introduced himself as Dr. Ernst Wilhelm, son of Dr. and Mrs. Wilhelm of Párkány-Nána, Hungary. My heart stood still. I had known him and his brother as little boys when his parents hosted Erwin and me in Prague. I never had the strength to get in touch with them again but had heard that Dr. Wilhelm died of the flu. Now young Ernst Wilhelm had been delegated to come all the way from Prague to offer help, and I asked him to take my jewelry to my parents [yes, this has consequence]. How far the news of Jakob's death in Dachau had spread!

On another occasion, Rosa came in with a young man who had asked for our apartment at the superinten-dent's. It was the Dutchman Knook [the reformed Nazi sympathizer], whom we had met in the Alps. He had read about our tragedy and had come from Rotterdam to offer his help. He pleaded with me to come to Holland with Paul, that there was a powerful Jewish community there, that he was sure we could have a future there. I told him that we were still hostages, not free to leave [com-plete paperwork was essential], and promised to keep him informed of further developments. After he left, Rosa told me she was sure he was a spy [because he had Aryan looks and waited outside the apartment when Rosa refused him entry] and could not be convinced otherwise.

It was not easy to get a passport. It took many weeks before all the necessary papers were gathered. One had to line up before offices and wait for hours, only to be turned down [for any slight paperwork discrepancy]. Sofie knew of some individuals [fixers who waited in lines and generally knew the ropes] who, against good pay, did the job. To get a passport you had to submit an *Unbedenklichkeitserklärung* (clearance certificate). It was valid for a limited time only and available only when, in a nerve-wracking process, all kinds of official statements had been assembled. In our case, it was August when this goal was reached.

We had the affidavit and the permit of the Sochnut, the provisional government of Palestine. To be eligible to leave on the US quota we needed a temporary permit to wait in another country. [She could have left for Palestine but wanted to go to the US, which required both the affidavit from Siegmund Singer and a specific quota number not yet reached. A temporary permit or emergency visa would allow her to leave Austria right away.] Sometime in July I received a letter from Dr. Joshua Goldberg, one of the noted New York rabbis, who suggested a meeting. He had been delegated by the Zionist Council to provide emergency entries to the US in particularly threatened and noteworthy cases. He said he would take up our case when he returned to the US in September.

About the same time Emil Engel, chief secretary of the anti-Zionist faction of the Jewish community, called me to ask that I come to his office at Seitenstettengasse at a certain hour the next day to meet the British delegate of the Council of Deputies of British Jewry. He received me at the appointed hour. The interview lasted a few minutes, and within a week we had an emergency visa for England. It became the key to our future. A few days later I received the necessary papers and clearance certificate and informed Dr. Löwenherz.

Jakob's residence at 22 Weimarer Street
as marked in 2012. Photo by Julie Metz

Eye to Eye with Eichmann

August 1938

Irma was ready to acquire the final document needed for departure, a passport issued by Ostmark. She planned to send Paul first, then deal with her household and follow soon after.

Jews were leaving Austria at a rate of three to four thousand a month with assistance from Josef Löwenherz and others acting under Adolf Eichmann's cold command. Nazis contrived a bureaucratic maze designed to fleece Jews of their assets before departure. Capricious Viennese officials and red tape further slowed the process. Eichmann wanted more efficiency and better means of oversight. He consolidated all the emigration checkpoints in the confiscated palace of the Rothschilds, a dynastic banking family, and called it the Central Office for Jewish Emigration. Between the gold leaf–edged Tiepolo frieze on the ceiling and the exotic wood parquet floors of the palace ran long corridors of rooms stripped of the Rothschilds' artwork and furniture. There behind desks sat officials receiving the long queues of former Austrian citizens grasping the papers that might set them free or hold them back for some infraction such as failure to pay the dog tax. Irma's date at the Rothschild palace was on or near August 30, the day when Eichmann wrote to the Berlin security office about his accomplishment (as translated in the *Jewish Virtual Library*):

> The aim of the Central Office for Emigration is to force poor Jews to emigrate and to make the rich ones leave only if a number of poor Jews, proportionate to the rich Jews' capital, go as well.
>
> Prior to the creation of the Central Office, papers and passports were provided without differentiation. The first Jew to come received documents regardless of his emigration prospects. The result was that the papers would often expire while the Jews still had no possibility to emigrate. The police department document and the certificate of tax payment are good for only four weeks. These Jews had to go through the same process several times until they could emigrate. This caused heavy workloads for the authorities.
>
> The Central Office for Emigration supplies the paperwork and passports only to those Jews who can emigrate. Many Jews hold visas that are valid for a limited time only. To prevent these visas from expiring, they are given top priority. The Jewish political organizations are looking for emigration possibilities for Jews. The period when Jews emigrated in groups is over; one has to concentrate on individual emigration. The Central Office prepares two hundred Jews for emigration daily by supplying them with passports and supervising their departure.
> Heil Hitler,
> Eichmann

About two hundred thousand Austrian Jews were in urgent need of a place to go. Britain and America were accepting thirty thousand Germans and Austrians a year, while Palestine took ten or fifteen thousand. Josef Löwenherz had attended a conference in Évian, France, organized to encourage increases in international immigration quotas to meet the crisis. Thirty-two of the thirty-three delegations, including America's, failed to increase quotas. A poll by *Fortune* magazine in the July 1938 edition found that fewer than 5 percent of Americans wanted to welcome more. In heroic defiance of his superior diplomat in Nazi Berlin, Chinese Consul-General Ho Feng-Shan in Vienna would quietly issue up to four thousand visas to Shanghai.

As Jakob's widow, Irma had special attention from his sympathetic colleagues, including Jakob's onetime anti-Zionist rival Engel, who arranged her visa for England. By this time, all Jewish factions were aligned with Zionist leaders in the same way that there are no atheists in foxholes. Irma was lucky in having options, as many would-be refugees had none at all. She had emergency visas for Palestine and England—meaning welcome in both for temporary shelter pending an offer of permanent residence. She preferred England for Paul as well as herself, if possible. Her US affidavit from Siegmund Singer, signed after he withdrew the first when Jakob died, offered permanent residence in America but was valid only after a place opened up under the American quota—about a year away, according to Löwenherz's information circulars.

Irma resumes her narrative in late August 1938:

I

It took some time until I was given a date at the Rothschild palace, where I was supposed to get Paul's passport. I was not at all prepared, nor could I have anticipated what was in store for me.

Early that morning I was there. I was given a receipt for having paid our Kultus tax [to fund Jewish welfare and emigration]. I added it to the other collected papers. Then I was told I had to wait until Eichmann came. He had given orders he wanted to be present when I was there. It took a long time before I was told he had arrived. I did not see him. I was given an escort named Dr. L. Friedmann. [We will call him LF, because he is not the Leopold Friedmann already mentioned.] He led me to narrow stairs in the rear of the building, which led to a door on the first floor. People were lined up from the first to the last step.

They grumbled when LF tried to lead me up. When he said I was Jakob Ehrlich's widow, they silently made room for me. The stairs were narrow, used in normal times by servants and tradespeople. The door at the top of the stairs opened. We stood in the first of a succession of rooms. In each there were several desks in a row with officials representing certain offices. There was a line before the first. We had to wait.

There had been a buzzing of voices. Suddenly there was a deadly silence, and it seemed as though the waiting people had stiffened. LF whispered: "Eichmann is here." He was walking up and down behind our backs while we were standing before the desks. People did not know what it meant. I was cool and petrified as I was at times of great anxiety. I acted as though it did not mean a thing to me. I did not look at him.

My turn at the first table came. The passport form was to be filled out. That day, for the first time, the names of the transit countries before reaching one's goal had to be entered. I thought hard. End destination: USA. We had a permit for Palestine. Prague—I hoped to stay with my parents, sister, and family for a while. England. That left two countries through which I had to pass from Bohemia, namely Germany and Holland. These six countries were entered.

Next table, waiting in line, and confirmation of taxes paid. At times I was told that Eichmann was gone. And then he reappeared again. A paper was missing—the tax for a dog had not been paid. We did not have a dog. "*Und schon?*" ("So what?") "What do I have to do? My clearance certificate is about to expire." "Never mind. Pick up your papers at the next desk." I stood numbly at the entrance to the third room. LF took my hand and led me in. "What do you want?" asked the man at the third desk. "I was told to pick up my papers." "Name?" He handed me two passports. I didn't understand and was about to ask. "Don't ask," he said.

LF dragged me through a small door to the enormous foyer, squeezed my hand and said, "*Viel Glück*" ("Good luck"), closed the door, and disappeared. I found myself alone in a huge, dim place, on top of the wide, stately staircase. The curtains at the floor-to-ceiling windows were drawn, hiding the view of the park behind the palace. I was holding two passports in my hand, bewildered, trying to figure out what it all meant, when I heard steps. I saw Eichmann in black uniform, slowly coming up. I started descending, thinking, *What do you want from me? You may take my life. I don't mind. But let my child go.* We passed each other, eye to eye. No word was spoken.

I reached the ground floor. Somebody opened the large main entrance. Dr. Reik, LF, and another man were anxiously waiting for me. I was told it took six hours before I reappeared. The other man asked excitedly whether I had thrown myself at Eichmann's feet and implored him to let us go.

....

What happened? By all appearances, Eichmann himself had ordered a passport for Irma when she had applied only for Paul's, and then stalked the halls to make sure she got it. Irma made up her own reasons for the inexplicable. Knowing that Eichmann had a watch on her after Jakob's funeral, she fixed him with her icy stare in that stairwell and concluded that her hauteur had something to do with it.

Irma's pride is telling, but she was wrong. Historian Doron Rabinovici, author of *Eichmann's Jews*, helps to unravel a scenario. Under Eichmann's orders, Löwenherz was negotiating with Jewish organizations overseas to fund forced emigrations for the poor. In that timeframe, Löwenherz secured $50,000 a month from abroad. Irma's passport was probably a condition from Jews in London or America. That would explain why Eichmann stalked the halls of the Rothschild palace while Irma was there: to prevent petty bureaucrats from scuttling his secret deal through demand for, say, a dog tax receipt. Jakob was right: Irma was a high-value hostage. Passing Irma on the Rothschild's elegant staircase, Eichmann may have been congratulating himself on his extortionate money deal.

I wonder about the date of his bragging memo to Berlin: August 30. The Central Office had been operating for about two weeks. Could he also have been tracking a known person through his streamlined operation before he reported on its efficiency to Berlin? If so, he learned that it took six hours, not counting queuing time.

She wrote:

2

Up to then I had not thought it possible to leave at the same time as Paul. He could have left earlier when Professor and Mrs. Levy agreed to take care of him in Cambridge, but then I had wanted to wait for Jakob to come home. Now I was free to go as well, but nothing was prepared for a complete breakaway.

There was the possibility of going to Palestine. I went to pick up our permit, which I had deposited at the Palestine Office [for safekeeping], as instructed by ambassador Kendrick. Director Rothenberg, husband of an old friend [Krassny], told me brazenly that the permit was not there. It had been sold [or he sold it, as Irma believed].

I had hoped we would be able to remain in Europe near my parents, my sister, and her family, but the political situation was getting more dangerous every day. I adored English culture. America was so far away and it frightened me. I didn't have enough money for America. I went to the main office of the airlines to secure passage to London and was told that we would have to wait three weeks before we could get tickets. One seat was available for September 22, but Paul refused to go alone. There were two seats available for September 23, but only if I paid the fare from Istanbul, to which I agreed [she paid for the extra leg on the flight route].

One day a Gestapo arrived at our apartment and asked for the script of Jakob's famous speech. It had found wide publicity, courageously denouncing the National Socialists and discrimination against Jews and pleading for the naturalization of Jews who had fled from Galicia to Vienna before the Russian invasion. In the consternation of the moment, I told the Gestapo the papers had already been handed to someone who had previously come to fetch them. [This was a lie. They were hidden in Rosa's apartment.]

From the time I applied for our tickets until departure I arranged for passage of our furniture to England [still subject to appropriation; fortunately the young man from Prague had taken her jewelry to her parents in Czechoslovakia]. Officials came to inspect the shipment and confiscated our Spitzweg and Alt paintings but approved the rest.

Ellie Friedmann [wife of imprisoned Zionist Desider Friedmann] and I had become friends. The former fun-loving woman [*pläsier-fisch*, or pleasure-fish] was a person of noble character [and was helping others leave when she could not]. There were always visitors in their huge apartment. Once when I was there I met a friend of the Friedmann family, Mr. Graubart. He was about to leave for England, said he had been an admirer of Jakob's, and said he would meet us when we arrived in London. I did not take the promise seriously.

Ellie told me that she and her husband had dinner with a Mr. Cohen a few months ago. He was a Lithuanian emigrant turned rich businessman who owned a chain of department stores in London. He had invited them to call on him if they came to England. His son-in-law, Barnett Janner, was a member of parliament (MP). Ellie knew that wealthy emigrants sought Barnett Janner's intervention and legal help in England, and said she would write and ask them to take care of us. I soon forgot about that [in the chaos of the moment].

Ellie insisted I equip myself for England and possibly the US. I would not be able to take money out anyway, so it would be better to spend it usefully. For me it seemed important to have a fine new coat, a winter suit, and two black-and-white silk dresses made by Ellie's dressmaker. Since Jakob's death, I had worn only black mourning dresses, as was the custom in Europe. Paul was invited to be outfitted by Mr. Lowy, owner of Vienna's most elegant men's store, who went to London twice a year to equip members of the royal family. Mr. Lowy took Paul's measurements for a sports jacket and for the then-fashionable plus fours, a fine blue winter coat, and a blue suit.

Paul was with his friends most of the time. Many of ours had already left. I said goodbye to Erna Patak, and to Richard Beer-Hofmann, author of the drama *Jakob's Traum* and the famous poem "Lullaby for Miriam." He was still in a state of shock after a brutal search of his villa by Gestapo hoodlums the day before. Bernhard Altmann was trying to get him an emergency visa to the US. One of my last visitors was Sigmund Freud's widowed sister. She read me his letter describing his honorary reception in Paris, and then London.

3

On our last day in Vienna, there was the first blackout [an order to block lights for a possible air raid]. Rosa was with us. The curtains were drawn. We sat in the dimly lighted *Herrenzimmer* (study). Few people knew of our departure.

Early the next morning LF came to accompany us to the airport. We were saying goodbye to Rosa near the entrance door when the bell rang. A letter from the Gestapo was delivered, ordering me to Gestapo head-quarters the next morning.

LF came with us by taxi to the airport. The first thing was to show the permit for the thirty schillings [about three hundred dollars in today's money] each of us was allowed to take out of the country. I had not applied for it, since I would have had to submit our passports and feared that somebody might interfere, or that Eichmann might reconsider. Consequently all of my money was confiscated. Paul had to undergo a body search, and our nicely packed belongings were thrown out of the luggage and then stuffed back in.

Irma wrote of the Gestapo summons, "Had I gone, I may not have returned from that interrogation. Paul might have been taken care of by the Löwenherzes, who would have tried to get him to Palestine with Youth Aliyah." Eichmann's passport deal could have been undermined by the Gestapo, who were not under Eichmann's direct command. Sometimes they toyed with people rather than serve Eichmann's policy of emigration. They had asked for the text of Jakob's speech and may have caught Irma in a lie. She had not given it to another policeman as she said. Whatever the reason for it, a summons to the Gestapo did not bode well.

4

We were ready to embark. I think there were fifty-six passengers. I was numb. That we were departing without money did not seem to affect me. I had planned to stay with my parents for some time before going on to England, but the threats of the political situation had made it impossible. We were to land briefly in Prague, and I thought my family would be there to lend me money.

It was our first flight. Paul was sick. *Luftlöcher* (air holes), the stewardess explained. Prague: I see my parents; Edna and Fritz with Lilly, Hannah, and John [sister, her husband, and Paul's three cousins]; our friends Anny and engineer Emil Ehrhardt; and my dear cousins Anna Reiman and Edith at a distance, behind a rope, prevented by two soldiers from meeting us. My mother pleaded with them. Suddenly I saw my parents, escorted by the soldiers, approaching us. They alone were allowed to say goodbye to us. While my mother was embracing me, she slipped a parcel [see "Appraisal" section] into my hand. We were not allowed to speak. My parents had to leave. From afar I saw the others waving.

The moment my parents were leaving, an airplane arrived behind us. Out stepped Löwenherz and Rothenberg [the dealer in stolen passports to Palestine, Irma thought]. They were returning from London where, under Eichmann's orders, they had been negotiating with Jewish leaders for funds to hasten the emigration of the Jews of Vienna. Dr. Löwenherz waved and shouted over to us, "The Janners are inviting you." It did not mean a thing to me.

We flew over Germany. Next stop: Rotterdam. The Dutchman Knook was waiting for us. How could he have heard of our arrival? He treated us to tea and cookies and brought a box of candies. He pleaded with me to remain in Holland. He had talked to leaders of the Jewish community and was sure I would find a rewarding job. I still have the snapshots he made of us. We parted. Knook's loyalty had been moving.

Last stretch—water, then beautiful meadows and estates. We were approaching London. I was emotionally drained and did not know what to expect or what I was to do. We landed. We dragged our luggage, since we had no money for porters. I gave the stewardess Knook's box of candy, one piece less to carry. We were the last ones to come before the immigration officer. Where were we going? Was there somebody to meet us? I had been told that somebody of the Woburn House [the chief Jewish agency to help refugees] would be there. The officer asked whether I wanted to telephone somebody, but I had no money and did not know anybody. He asked whether I could not think of anybody else who might have come to meet us. I thought, Why does he ask? Had I known, I would have told him.

Just then I remembered the name of Graubart, who had said at Ellie Friedmann's that he would come to the airport when we arrived in London. Just to say something, I gave his name. He was called. His name resounded in the large, empty waiting hall, and he came running. There had been some difficulties with the car a friend had lent him. He got the receipt for Paul's camera, which had been confiscated because we were unable to pay the import tax. While leading us to the car, he told us that Mr. Janner, an MP, lawyer, and president of the Board of Jewish Deputies, and his wife, Elsie, had invited us to spend the first few days with them. Ellie had told me she had written to them some time ago, but I had forgotten about it.

We arrived at 3 Lancaster Terrace, opposite Hyde Park. The door opened, and there we stood in a warmly lighted room with two friendly people, and a boy and a girl. Paul was fifteen years old, Greville Janner was ten, his sister, Ruth, five. Later, Elsie Janner said that she had been amazed to see two tall people [Irma and Paul]—she herself was small—who stood there and did not move. It was all so unreal. A short while later Paul was sitting on the floor playing Monopoly with Greville, little Ruth watching. I was shown to my own room with an adjacent bath and a bunch of beautiful red roses on a desk.

....

Thousands of Austrian Jews survived because Josef Löwenherz and others expedited emigration and stayed on in agony as forced emigration was replaced by deportations to camps and ghettos, some of which became killing fields in 1942. But such things were inconceivable then, even though unimaginable things were already happening.

Irma and Paul came very close to being trapped in Austria. Their flight on September 23, 1938, was the last before mid-November. Nazis halted flights the next day to secure borders as Hitler met with British prime minister Neville Chamberlain and learned that Britain would not intervene against an invasion of Czechoslovakia. A week later, on October 1, German troops occupied the Czech zones where Germans lived, the coveted Sudetenland. If Irma had booked a later flight, and if she had not abandoned the idea of visiting her parents in Czechoslovakia before England, they might have been stuck.

Another scenario makes my skin creep. Irma's friends Ellie Friedmann and Sofie Löwenherz, wives of Jakob's Zionist colleagues, stayed on with their husbands as Nazi policy grew more brutal over the next months and years. If Jakob had been alive, she would not have received the second passport for herself and might have stayed on trying to help her husband. Emigration was close to impossible after June of 1941. In his early death, he may have saved her life.

Many other things could have gone wrong. If Jakob's estate had not been settled by the judge who happened to return to his office before going on vacation, all would have been delayed by a fateful month. If she had depended on the visa to Palestine that was stolen by Rothenberg or his allies, she would have been trapped. If she had accepted Knook's invitation to stay in Holland, she might have been in the same danger as Anne Frank was four years later in 1942. Those who stayed in Europe were not safe for long. Eight of the eleven well-wishers who saw Irma and Paul off at Prague airport on September 23, 1938, were doomed by events yet to unfold in the 1940s.

Later Irma understood that the box of candy from Knook, which she gave to a stewardess when it was too much to carry, was probably filled with cash. In due course, we will learn what was contained in the packet smuggled across the cordon at Prague airport by Irma's mother, Karla.

Once Irma had belonged in Vienna as a German Jewish woman, and now she belonged nowhere: only defiant self-possession and a community led by Zionists supported her. Right up to her late August ordeal at the passport office, Irma had thought single-mindedly about saving Paul and might not have saved herself—but for the Jewish community's care. By Buddhist reckoning she had suffered the end of a life with Erwin, and the end of a life with Jakob, and earned a considerable awakening in compassion. Her life had another karmic whirl to go. She left Austria a free woman: free of rights, free of most possessions, free of money. Somehow, she found herself with Paul in a welcoming home in the heart of London, where she had always wanted to go.

....

Fifty-nine years after my grandfather's death, on a showery day in June of 1997, I took the #71 streetcar to the Zentralfriedhof cemetery on the outskirts of Vienna with my father, Paul, to visit the place where Jakob Ehrlich lies buried. A large gray stone sarcophagus commissioned by Irma covers the plain marker laid by the Jewish Community under Nazi menace. The huge trees nearby have matured since they sheltered Irma and Paul on a similar day in May of 1938, when they stood at Jakob's funeral alongside the smirking Adolf Eichmann and the tormented Josef Löwenherz.

Irma would later be told that a guard inflicted mortal blows on Jakob at Dachau when he did not break stone like a younger man. He died a symbol of Jewish pride and self-determination. Viennese Jews in London, Palestine, and New York mourned the freedom fighter Jakob Ehrlich; my father's tears and mine did not fall for a martyr. They fell for the husband of Irma and father of Paul.

I take comfort in knowing that Jakob died unaware that remaining Jews would be deported into camps and ghettos around 1940, and that death camps would be invented in 1942. We would not have wished on Jakob the suffering of his political colleagues Desider Friedmann and Robert Stricker, who saw those horrors firsthand. Like Martin Luther King and Moses before him, Jakob led his people as far as he could and saw the Promised Land.

Irma's London residence, 1939 and 2017

Sink or Swim

Late 1938–July 1939

B lack London taxicabs and red double-decker buses whizzed along Bayswater Road in late September 1938, discharging passengers bound on one side for the gold-hued autumnal grace of Kensington Gardens and on the other for a phalanx of white-columned stone townhouses called Lancaster Terrace. Behind the middle door of the five-door facade, at number three, lived the Janner family: Barnett (Barney) and Elsie, and their children, Greville and Ruth. There amidst burnished Victorian wainscoting and draping folds of chintz, Irma and Paul found warmth and welcome after a day spent dodging the Gestapo, bidding a last farewell to family in Prague, touching down in Rotterdam, and landing penniless and bewildered at Croydon Airport.

In September of 1938, Barney Janner was a candidate for reelection to the House of Commons and Elsie was a magistrate and an engaged political wife, as Irma had been. Irma had forgotten that her friend Ellie Friedmann said she would write to a British political contact on her behalf, and blanked on the name when Josef Löwenherz called across the tarmac in Prague, "The

157

Janners are inviting you." Irma and Paul had landed in a Zionist haven hosted by the Janners.

Zionism had hatched in Vienna but had spread its wings in England on the strength of support from elites. British foreign secretary Lord Balfour's declaration of 1917 had promised a "national home for the Jewish people" in Palestine, and English Lord Rothschild had merged his privately funded sanctuary there into the future homeland. Britain ran the League of Nations' Mandate to administer Palestine, with Sir Herbert Samuel, former Liberal Party leader, as Mandatory Palestine's first governor. Baron Israel Moses Sieff, Michael Marks of the Marks & Spencer department stores, and Josiah Wedgwood of the porcelain manufacturer supported Zionism. Russian-born biochemist and leader of the World Zionist Organization, Chaim Weizmann, who had given visibility to the younger Jakob Ehrlich at the 1925 conference in Vienna, resided in England and spoke to power there.

Britain's influential Zionists had been busy organizing aid for Jews from Germany, and then Austria in the 1930s, while the British government sized up Hitler. As Irma and Paul left Vienna, Prime Minister Neville Chamberlain was ceding the German-speaking Sudetenland border between Germany and Czechoslovakia to Hitler, hoping German unification would appease him. "Peace in our time," Chamberlain told the war-weary British public. In early October of 1938, one week after Irma and Paul arrived in London, Hitler's armies occupied the Sudetenland with a German welcome like the one in Vienna. Irma's family waited nervously to see whether Hitler would break yet another promise and invade the remainder of Czechoslovakia where they lived, as did the British government.

Up to this time in her life, Irma had seen refugees as Eastern European Jews ridiculed for their religious taboos, foreign habits, and improper German. But in London, refugees were Central European Jews whose German habits and improper English made them just as awkward. Irma, the English language major, was exceptional. The woman who performed on a chair as a tot and starred as fairy queen Titania at Deutsches Haus was about to audition for a make-or-break role on a formidable English stage.

Irma recalled:

I

The scene we found ourselves in at the Janners' lighted living room in the heart of London seemed completely unreal, like a fantasy. I could not have imagined how suddenly we would find a new way of life. (Greville Janner remembered this encounter in his 2003 memoir, *To Life!)*

Our problems were to get Paul to school as fast as possible and for me to find a job. The first morning we got up at our usual hour. Everybody was asleep, including the staff. We left the house and crossed the street to Hyde Park with scarcely any people, hoboes sleeping on benches, and sheep grazing on the beautiful meadows. Paul said the flight from Vienna had been short, only six hours [the time it took to go through the Central Office for Jewish Emigration], and here we were in a different world. We strolled across the lawns—no fines for stepping on the grass as there would have been in a public park in Vienna. We returned to the house and our first breakfast of scrambled eggs and kippers. Elsie and Barney got up late after a meeting the night before and rushed off, Elsie driving.

It was Erev Rosh Hashanah [Jewish New Year's Eve], and we were invited to Elsie's parents' stately mansion at Bishop's Gate [Elsie's father was heir to the department store chain that later purchased Selfridges]. A liveried driver in a Rolls-Royce came to pick us up with Barney and Elsie. As Paul sat down next to the driver, he turned back and said to me, "Not half bad for a start." There were prayers, ancient ritual songs, and then a rich kosher meal served by the parlor maid, followed, at 10 p.m., by the first television I had ever seen.

The day after the holidays, Elsie took me to the Woburn House [a center for Jewish aid organizations]. There was feverish activity with the problems of the refugees. A Mrs. Schwab was the almighty person who placed teenage boys and girls in schools. Lines of waiting people were everywhere. When Mrs. Schwab saw Elsie, she waved her forward, and we had an immediate interview. She had a suggestion for Paul. In Broadstairs there was a house being made ready for boys, mostly from Germany, who were to live there with their teachers. I do not know where I found the courage. I said that Paul spoke English, and I did not want him to speak German and have the lifelong stigma of an accent. I wanted Paul educated in an English school and without loss of time. We left, the problem unsolved. Fortunately, Elsie understood my argument.

The next day a telephone call came in. Elsie told me that Dr. Vera Weizmann had invited me to afternoon tea in honor of Jakob's memory. Dr. Weizmann, physician wife of World Zionist Organization president Chaim Weizmann, was co-founder of the Women's International Zionist Organization. She moved in the highest British society. Elsie was impressed.

A butler announced my arrival at the elegant Weizmann home. Dr. Chaim Weizmann came to greet me, and then I was alone with Mrs. Weizmann. We had tea and a long conversation. Suddenly she asked whether I had done any public speaking. I said that I had taught. *She said I had a gift to make one feel what I said.* She said I might find employment with the Women's International Zionist Organization, and that she would let me try out with some of her friends—names of great renown, to my horror. If that failed, she would try for a job in the staff welfare department of Marks & Spencer through her friends.

Then we discussed Paul's problem [school]. She had an idea: she would ask her friend Sir Wyndham Deedes [former secretary to the first governor of Palestine under Britain, Sir Herbert Samuel] whether he could get a scholarship for Paul at Brighton College. A few days later, she called to say that the headmaster was so pleased with a refugee recommended previously by Deedes that he was willing to give another boy a chance. Paul was accepted, and everything was free. I only had to provide the clothes from a special store. [Irma secured 8 percent of Jakob's deposit in the Austrian Postal Savings Bank, a sum she could retrieve in London because of international banking oversight. She also secured £150 of back salary owed to Jakob as administrator of the Keren Kayemeth Fund, because the fund's purse strings were in London.]

To have gained a scholarship for Brighton seemed a fantastic stroke of luck, bitter as it would be to part with Paul. Our friend Emil Krassny had taken his son and Theodor Herzl's grandson to a school there three or four years earlier. The Janners were jubilant. Early one morning we took the train to Brighton. I watched Paul disappear behind the entrance, knowing I was giving him over to life. He never looked back.

2

My interview with the Weizmanns changed my situation at the Janners. Their hospitality had been meant to last for a few days. With Paul at Brighton getting a first-rate education and me traveling as a speaker for Youth

Aliyah, the Janners invited me to stay on as a long-term guest. [Youth Aliyah resettled Jewish refugee children in Palestine. Irma had thought even Paul might need it if the Gestapo took her.] Elsie and Barney disapproved of my meeting with "the refugees" at the house [a distinction between German-speaking outsiders and Irma]. Their view was that I spoke English and was set to become British. Understandably, their children were not to know of the catastrophe in Europe.

Most of the people who sought refuge in England did not speak English. I was fluent and had taught Paul, and this was decisive in our acceptance. Though I had a university degree, rare for a woman at the time, I had not yet been to England. It had been my fervent desire to hear and speak the language there. It gave me confidence. Deep down, I was frightened and lost, and felt an impenetrable darkness. I had no idea there were welfare organizations. I had a terrible pride about accepting financial help and declined every offer. I preferred to work hard. All that followed stood in sharp contrast to what a refugee—a term I did not know—could expect. In spite of my anxieties, a new world opened. There were new challenges, and so many new things to see. I had a lot to learn. Elsie and Barney made it possible for me under the most favorable conditions.

The news of my being with the Janners spread like wildfire in Viennese Jewish circles. Mail was slipped under the entrance door five times a day, the first at seven a.m. I always found heaps of it from friends and other people begging for help or intervention for jobs or visas. I knew it was impossible to help, and it made me terribly unhappy.

3

That fall, my apprenticeship as a speaker began. Members of the board of directors of the Women's International Zionist Organization took me to parlor meetings at the homes of financiers and nobility. My role was to win people over to the great children's rescue work of Youth Aliyah [resettlement in Palestine, supported by the Women's International Zionist Organization]. I was accompanied to every meeting by the best orators with great names and had to live up to each occasion. I was in deep mourning, and the glare of limelight put a heavy strain on me. But I was severe with myself: *If you don't swim, you will sink, and your boy with you.* Somehow it worked. I was successful and made many friends.

By the end of November, I was asked to go to Montreal in the company of Ethel Hayman, a wealthy South African socialite, to address a big meeting.

....

In a single week, Irma pole-vaulted from bereft refugee status to glamorous speaker in Britain's social stratosphere, plucking an elite scholarship for Paul on the way up. One can't call it luck. Her husband's martyrdom, violent expulsion from her rightful home, a haunted stumble through a Nazi labyrinth to arrive robbed and alien in temporary shelter—that isn't lucky. Yet don't call it victimhood. Her martyred husband's fame, her social refinement, and tea and sympathy with a talent scout right when she needed a role—that is not the trajectory of a victim. Yet her attitude—that refusal to give in to victimhood—her dignity, perseverance, and self-respect—these qualities told the English women that she was one of their own.

Vera Weizmann's words "You have the gift to make one feel" clue me in to something else. Amidst a crisis of overwhelming proportions, Irma had a way of motivating people to look rather than turn away, and to personify hope. Irma's storytelling voice reached outside of herself and made people want to help. She had the potential to bring in donations.

Irma had linked directly to a powerful network of Zionist women. That generation of women turned their social connections and intelligence to the high calling of philanthropy in the 1930s and 1940s while their husbands acted in men-only business and political circles. In Irma they had a woman with deep knowledge of Zionism and its rhetoric, a classical education, and an electrifying personal story, combined with personal charm and steel, and the evocative gifts of a born storyteller. And she could express it all in good English, even if "wonderful" began with a "v."

Irma told her story to the epic tune of Zionism: of a people's oppression and flight, of wandering in the wilderness, of holding on to dignity and hope, of helping one's own, of not succumbing to victimhood. She let her audience see how they could reach out a hand to save a child from persecution and death.

Those remarkable outward-looking Zionist women had figured out that Canada was an untapped market for donations, and that appeals on behalf of children might unlock resources. Canada was disengaged at political levels, anti-war, and hardly accepting any Jewish immigrants. Canada's Jewish population had arrived a generation or two earlier after pogroms in Eastern Europe, and had assimilated fully as North Americans. Would Irma Ehrlich's words connect them emotionally to the European Jewish crisis? Zionist women placed a bet on Irma when they scheduled a fundraising tour in Canada for Irma to be accompanied by South African socialite Ethel Hayman in the last week of December 1938.

In early November, the German terrorist spree known as Kristallnacht destroyed hundreds of synagogues and thousands of Jewish businesses, killed and maimed, and sent thirty thousand Jewish men to concentration camps. German authorities and Catholic clergy had encouraged and participated in the mob violence. The world woke up to Hitler's potential. Britain had been rebuilding the country after World War I and resisted the idea of spending on military rearmament. Few wanted to raise immigration quotas for refugees. Parliament responded to the humanitarian crisis innovatively, by allowing entry for Jewish children up to the age of seventeen traveling without parents or visas—on the Kindertransport—for placement in foster homes.

On Christmas Day of 1938, after a rough week's ocean passage to Montreal and a full day of nonstop socializing capped by a formal dinner, and after introductory remarks by Samuel Bronfman [Seagram Company Ltd. spirits] and Ethel Hayman, Irma stood in fear at the podium of the Mount Royal Hotel, looking out at a sea of six hundred faces. A successful fundraising speech would mean a three-month, three-thousand-mile train odyssey from Montreal to Vancouver; the alternative—if she did not get the part—was shame. Irma had obsessed over how to start her speech without having come to a decision. She heard herself start talking and then felt her confidence surge. Total silence in the room confirmed that the audience was hers. When the last of the people moved by her speech ebbed away from her side, an exhausted Irma retired to her room and vomited her anxiety and relief.

Irma and Ethel Hayman headed out the next day, stopping at large cities and any whistle-stop town where a quorum of Jewish émigrés had gathered. They rolled across the plains in velvety first-class train cars, stayed in the homes of wealthy naturalized Canadians or the hotels they owned, toured the spectacular Rocky Mountains by sleigh, and looked out over Niagara Falls into the United States. Irma wondered when her name would come to the top of the American quota queue, and whether the forested country across the waterfall would be her future home.

She wrote:

4

I returned to London on March 15, 1939. Hitler's troops were marching on Prague [after taking the Sudetenland]. My family was there. I found a letter from my mother saying their interest payment had not arrived [despite Irma's attempt to secure the investment, her parents' life savings were stolen by someone who knew they were Jewish]. That same night I wrote to my family begging them to leave immediately. I would rent a house, and my brother-in-law Fritz Werner could find work as a correspondent since he knew nine languages. Edna could take care of our parents, her children, and Paul when I was traveling. My parents replied: "*Alte Bäume verpflanzt man nicht*" ["One does not transplant old trees," a German saying]. Fritz wrote that he could not face exile from home again after his six years captive in Siberia. I should get their children to England—how? The rest of them would subsist on his pension until the Hitler tide blew over.

Brighton College had seemed the peak of all expectations. When Paul told me how unhappy he was there, it was an awful shock [he complained of sexual misconduct at the school]. I spoke to Elsie about the situation and wanted her to reveal it to the headmaster. Elsie said I was naive—he knew about it, the same happened in many English and French colleges, and I, a refugee, certainly could not complain. I tried to get Paul away from the college on Sundays whenever I could. Elsie and Barney were critical. It was "not British."

5

After my return from Canada in March 1939, nine times as many contributions as expected were collected. The Women's International Zionist Organization called a meeting for me to report on my mission for Youth Aliyah. The meeting was held in the ballroom of an elegant London club. The place was crowded with women of rank and title [including Madame Dorothy de Rothschild, Viscountess Beatrice Samuel, Viscountess Violet Reading, Edith Eder, Dr. Vera Weizmann, Lady Rebecca Sieff, Miriam Sacher, Mathilde Marks, and Dr. Celina Sokolov. See "Notable Names" section]. I was scared stiff. As I started talking I calmed completely and got the warmest response. The organization asked how they could show their appreciation. I requested that they grant a permit to Palestine for Jakob's nephew Dr. Hugo Deutsch in St. Pölten, Austria. [The permit was granted.]

A few days later there was a luncheon in my honor at the house of Viscountess Samuel with about twelve guests. I was impressed by the liveried footman who announced the names of guests as they entered. England was at the height of her power, and the menu came from all of her dominions. I was inscribed in the Golden Book of the Keren Kayemeth [a high honor for contributions to the homeland] by Canadian Hadassah, as the Women's International Zionist Organization was called there. The secretary who fixed speaking appointments started calling me "the best propagandist in the English language." There was talk of tours to South Africa, India, Australia, and New Zealand. I said I would travel only if there was no war because I would not agree to separation from Paul.

My life began to run on two levels. My career seemed assured, and I had never been so socially engaged. But underlying everything was the ever-present heartache for Jakob. I was always lonely, always missing Jakob and Paul, always trying to live up to Jakob's expectations. I longed for his "well done." It was his name that made it possible for me to meet with leading Zionists everywhere. I had the opportunities; the challenge was to live up to them in honor of his name and to build a future for Paul's sake. I would not have had the strength without Paul.

I saw and learned a lot. English people felt top-of-the-world and looked down on Americans. I met people of different classes, from different countries and ways of life, and my views expanded. The miracle was that I was accepted.

During the next months [March–July 1939] I was very busy. I held parlor meetings in private homes to which printed invitations were sent out, and I traveled all around the country. I recall visits to Edinburgh, Glasgow, Newcastle upon Tyne, Birmingham, Liverpool, Manchester, York, and particularly Leicester and Leeds, because they became very important. Leicester was Barney Janner's constituency, and I met some of his and Elsie's friends there. After a big meeting in Leicester, everybody wanted to talk to me. Some of the women suggested trying to bring endangered Jewish young people to England, to find homes for the children, and place the older girls in households and hospitals. I gave them a list of names, including many from the SOS letters I received daily from Vienna and Prague.

I topped the list with my sister's children, Lilly, Hannah, and John Werner; the strikingly beautiful children of my cousin Vali Sinek Kopperl; my favorite cousin Anna's daughter, Edith Reiman; and Jakob's niece [Schrötter]. Hannah Werner was the first to be picked by a Mrs. Joseph, who had a daughter Hannah's age.

Somebody said, "One does not separate twins" [Hannah and John were fourteen-year-old twins], and Mrs. Millet, a wealthy woman, volunteered for John. They thought Edith Reiman could be placed at a hospital office and Jakob's niece in a household. [After a talk in Leeds, Irma's society escort Madame de Rothschild offered help for one person. Irma asked for help for her sister Edna's seventeen-year-old daughter, Lilly. On another occasion she secured a visa to New Zealand for her cousin's daughter, Edith Reiman.]

The Leicester meeting was in April or early May. Hannah and John Werner arrived in June. When I came to get them they were in a big hall with other children of the Kindertransport sitting on long brown benches. They looked like frightened birds. Each had a tablet with their name and a number strung around their necks. People came to pick and choose.

British homes took in ten thousand unaccompanied minors to varying levels of warmth and comfort. Eichmann had opened a second Central Office for Jewish Emigration in Prague. Parents in Germany, Austria, and Czech lands bid goodbye to teenagers and small children they would otherwise not have allowed to walk home from school alone. Irma's family in Czech lands took comfort in knowing that Irma was watching over Paul's cousins Hannah and John Werner.

Irma in Geneva, August 1939

Paul's Choice

Late 1939–1940

Freed up by Paul's school holiday in August of 1939, Irma and Paul joined Irma's South African friend Ethel Hayman on her drive to Geneva for the twenty-first World Zionist Congress. Ethel, Irma's escort on the Canada tour, had offered them this chance to refresh and reconnoiter in snowy Alpine heights. They ferried across the English Channel and cruised in Ethel's Rolls-Royce through five hundred miles of pretty French countryside, then swerved north near Lyon across the Swiss border and up into Geneva. Paul, sixteen, was lean and six feet tall if counting the two inches of dark hedge growing up top. Irma, nearly forty-nine, took along her black karakul overcoat, which made her look as bulky and important as Khrushchev, and a pillbox hat with plume and veil for stepping out at the Congress.

Paul and Irma were stateless at this time, with Ostmark German passports marked "Jew" that would not allow them back to Austria, and emergency visas for a temporary stay in England. As a precaution, Irma acquired British traveling papers as formal permission for the trip. She wanted to get Paul away from travails at school. His grades were good and he played violin in the school orchestra, a record that might qualify him for a place at Cambridge or Oxford. He joked about the icy film over the washbasin on winter mornings and the nasty school food, and refused to touch lima beans for the rest of his life. But he kept some things to himself. In the British way, he stopped talking about predatory behaviors at school.

The Zionist Congress in Geneva would discuss responses to the boiling refugee crisis. Britain in 1939 was failing to find a middle way for Arabs and Jews to live in peace in Palestine. Three proposals for partition that could lead to a two-state solution had met with Arab revolt and a prohibition on Jewish land purchases. Delegates at the Congress argued over whether to run people into Palestine illegally in violation of quotas lowered to mollify Arabs or to stay the course of diplomatic advocacy for a durable peace, as World Zionist Organization President Chaim Weizmann urged.

After taking Prague, Hitler had changed his rallying call from German unification to lebensraum, or room to live: more territory under supreme German domination. With fears of ongoing German aggression confirmed, Britain and France made a pact to declare war if Germany invaded Poland, the country sandwiched between Germany and Russia. Negotiators secretly sought Russian cooperation in stopping Hitler dead in Poland. But talks stalled in mid-August because the Soviets insisted on keeping any part of Poland they occupied.

On August 24, 1939, rumors began to leak about a pact between Soviet foreign minister Vyacheslav Molotov and German foreign minister Joachim von Ribbentrop. Molotov had swiveled suddenly under Stalin's orders and agreed with Germany to invade and divide Poland.

Paul and Irma were hiking near the mountain village of Adelboden, east of Geneva, when news of the pact filtered in. Their Ostmark passports would render them German enemy nationals in case of war. They packed up immediately and motored back to Geneva to meet the Weizmanns at the World Zionist Congress so they could cross the Swiss–French border under his diplomatic protection the next day. Irma and Paul pondered the foolish risk they had taken to see their beloved Alps.

At the border a convoy of Rolls-Royces came to a stop. Chaim Weizmann stepped out and spoke genially to the French guards, who waved the whole party through. Ninety-five miles down the road at Lyon, the Weizmanns hosted luncheon at the famed Aux Trois Faisans and drove on toward Paris while Irma's party headed for the Channel crossing at Boulogne-sur-Mer.

She wrote:

I

When we approached the port there was an endless line of cars. There was an eerie sense of foreboding everywhere. After waiting for a long time, it became obvious we would not be able to make it to England that night. We tried Calais. There was another line of cars from the Continent, but not so formidable. We took a chance. A town drummer arrived, and people assembled around him. He proclaimed general mobilization [prelude to war]. Many cried; my heart sank. Would we be stuck [detained as enemy nationals] in France?

Finally around midnight we got on the boat, but the danger was not yet over. Just before sailing, I was called before the captain for an interview. I spoke to him in French and he let us stay on board. It was a beautiful moonlit night and the passage was smooth. In the small hours of my birthday, August 28, we reached Dover, found accommodations, and drove on to London early in the morning.

What a change there was in the Janner household! Elsie and Barney were surprised we had returned. They thought we'd be stuck in Switzerland or France. Everything was in upheaval as they prepared to move from the center of London to the outskirts, and send the children to Canada. The day after our arrival, we had our gas masks fitted on. A blimp began to soar over Hyde Park [with cables to deter attack by air].

Suddenly Lilly Werner [seventeen-year-old daughter of Irma's sister Edna] arrived, having left Prague in the nick of time. How quickly a word from Madame de Rothschild had saved a life! I had to send her on to Leicester right away, where she was to train as a nurse at a hospital. Paul returned to Brighton. On Sunday, September 3, 1939, war was declared.

"The 'Phoney War' was on," Irma said, using the English phrase for the months before British and German forces clashed. Red-and-white posters went up urging the British public to *Keep Calm and Carry On*. France and Britain mustered weapons and armies. German and Russian troops rampaged through Poland but did not invade Britain.

Irma relocated to Brighton but returned to London when German bombers did not come as feared. To her great relief, speaking assignments resumed after a short break, and she angled for a full-time job. An employment contract would put Irma and Paul on track for naturalization as British citizens, making them independent of their useless Ostmark passports.

Declaration of war between Britain and Germany brought an unannounced shift in Nazi policy toward Jews. Concentration camps were running out of space. The policy of forced emigration was replaced by a new phase of mass deportations to Poland under Adolf Eichmann's ruthless command. North of Prague at Terezín (Theresienstadt), Jewish prisoners were put to work enlarging the old fort into a work camp that would hold 150,000 Czech and Austrian Jews. In Vienna, the Central Office stopped processing Jewish passports. Josef Löwenherz was left mitigating mistreatment for some with no recourse but to aid in the deportation of others. Irma wrote:

2

The London Times brought horrifying news daily. Trains crammed with Jewish families began to roll eastward, to yet unknown destinations. By and by it became clear what was happening. Without food, water, or hygienic facilities, sealed wagons were moving toward the newly established ghettos in Krakow, Łódź, and Warsaw. My heart sank every day when a new load of SOS letters reached me.

Paul and Irma had been in England for fifteen months in December of 1939, when Paul joined Irma and the Janners at 3 Lancaster Terrace for school holidays. Not yet English or American, unassimilated from Austria and Germany, they belonged nowhere.

Unlike most with temporary visas, Irma and Paul were "set to become British," the Janners had said. Cards in English and German warned them: Achtung! Don't take a job without approval. Don't speak German in public. A German accent was an enemy accent. Irma's Austrian friends had trickled into London but could not get good jobs like hers. Irma could not take them into the Janner home because they were "the refugees," so she met them at museums and parks. The Immerglücks, Krassnys, Rosenbergs, Morgensterns, Lasters, Strausses, and Neubrunns arrived.

Irma had come to love Hampton Court, the Chelsea Flower Show, the British Museum . . . she walked through Hampstead Heath and the wonderful Kew Gardens. With MP Barney Janner she went politicking on Petticoat Lane, where poor Eastern European immigrants crowded, and entered the Houses of Parliament where she saw Winston Churchill and Clement Attlee. She watched British Mandate of Palestine officer Orde Wingate and Zionist leader David Ben-Gurion tussle over the future of Palestine. From her first day in England, Irma had been swept aloft among British elites of great power and purpose, where she wore Jakob's mantle with pride. She saw the noble side of Britain.

But Paul saw an unfair society based on birth, not merit. His impression of England took shape on the feral grounds of a British boarding school, where sexual misconduct was ignored by upper-class parents who gave their sons over to the school's authority. As a Jewish immigrant who played violin better than he did football, Paul had a rougher time than he let on to his mother. Worse than unheated rooms and bad food were the unscalable hierarchies that let seniors dominate younger boys. He blamed the British class system.

On January 1, 1940, Irma and Paul sat down to early breakfast before a day trip to visit Hannah and John Werner in their foster homes in Leicester. Two letters lay on a silver tray brought to table by the butler. One envelope was of high-quality stationery from Britain, the other a lightweight aerogram from abroad.

Irma opened the British one and felt a joyful release. Here was her contract to work as secretary to Dr. Chaim Weizmann, president of the World Zionist Organization—to legitimize herself and Paul as British, to fully use her language skills for a great cause, to enjoy status and security: to travel *and* make a home.

Next letter: the official US government notification of visas for Irma and Paul Ehrlich. Their quota numbers had come up. Here was an offer to start over in a foreign country with unknown job prospects and uncertain potential.

"Let's think it over," Irma said. Mother and son slipped out the black door of 3 Lancaster Terrace, down the four steps of the stately white-columned portico, past the iron fretwork fence and into the tube bound for the train station. Standing on the platform in a cold January fog, black trains puffing steam into the station's vaulted ceiling, Irma asked Paul what he wanted to do.

"I'll never be English," he said, knowing his mother hoped he would, that she loved England and its social elites, and that the offer of an exhilarating job and security lay before her.

"It is your future. You should decide," Irma said. If Paul wanted to be American rather than English, she would set her steely will to make it happen. But was more uncertainty in America what he really wanted?

"Why should we stay here and wait for Hitler to arrive?" he asked.

"That does it," Irma said.

After the holidays Paul did not go back to Brighton College. The headmaster gave him a recommendation saying, "Given a chance, he should go far." They took a flat in Golders Green, London, to prepare for departure. Irma's influential friends wrote to Hadassah, the Women's Zionist Organization affiliate in New York, to recommend her for work, and she wrote about her travel plans to the Springarn family, cousins through her father's sister, Mary Hütter Stein, in New Jersey. Hadassah had written back with what appeared to be a job offer of $120 a month, close to the median income in America in 1940.

Paul and Irma booked tickets on the SS *Samaria* out of Liverpool to zigzag across the Atlantic Ocean evading any unseen U-boats in March 1940—two months before the end of the "Phoney War" and Germany's advance on France. On March 13, 1940, Irma and Paul bundled up, stepped up to the ship's high prow in cold predawn light, and watched the Statue of Liberty glide into view.

"We stood in awe," Irma wrote, "each with our own thoughts."

Irma and Jennie Grossinger at Grossinger's resort

Irma's Pride

March 1940 onward

⊰⋅————⋅⊱

I remember the first time I entered Irma's apartment in Kew Gardens, New York, where she lived for thirty-six years. White lace curtains from a long-ago empire fluttered over parquet floors, and high on a wall an Irma-like girl in a wooden frame looked out over fairy-tale rooftops from a perch on Prague Castle. My siblings and I clambered over the red bentwood chairs where two Viennese policemen once sat waiting for Jakob to finish shaving and pack an "overnight" bag. We handled Tauchnitz books covered in chintz by Erwin and Irma Kolmar, and gazed at the treasures in her glass-fronted Biedermeier cabinet: Bohemian art glass bowls of red and blue, Viennese champagne glasses etched in white, lusterless Jewish objects saved from a bullet smelter by our grandfather Lieutenant Jakob Ehrlich. Irma served creamy fruit salad from a silver-edged crystal bowl and a lavish white mound called a Malakoff Torte sliced generously onto Meissen porcelain plates. To a six-year-old child from Hamden, Massachusetts, Grandma's world consisted entirely of wonders.

"She is a real grande dame," I used to hear people say, and conflated "Grandma" with "grande dame," as though everyone's grandma once lived in Prague, Vienna, and London, and worked full-time in Manhattan. I watched her captivate guests at my parents' table with tales of miraculous escapes, families reunited, and wealth rebuilt in America, and absorbed potency from the electric flow of her telling: hold on to your dignity; never give in to victimhood; a woman is powerful and wise. Be grand. *I didn't understand how much she had to lose to have so much.*

Starting over in America, Irma relied on her old friend Pride, in all its chameleon manifestations. Vain pride had snatched a red bandana from her head after nearly drowning in the Vltava; stubborn pride put a firm hand to her back and shoved her from provincial Plzeň to worldly Vienna after Erwin; swallowed pride made her approach Jakob after she had rejected him once. Haughty pride glared at Adolf Eichmann himself and would not show fear. Wounded pride swept her onstage before daunting audiences in honor of Jakob's memory. Loving pride made sure that Paul got the life he wanted in America, no matter what it cost her. Pride conquers fear; it goads you when you are bone-weary and taunts you when you hide. Yes, foolish pride sidetracks you sometimes. But you don't know how many friends you have in pride until you summon them all to survive.

....

Irma and Paul spent their first weeks in America as guests of Irma's father's sister, Mary Hütter Stein, who had migrated to New Jersey from Bohemia in the 1880s. They moved on to a boarding house on Broadway and Ninety-Third Street in Manhattan as Irma networked her way into a few speaking assignments. Irma's nest egg of $2000 was dwindling fast. Four months later Irma chose the apartment at 118-14 Eighty-Third Avenue in Kew Gardens, Queens, for the tall trees and separation from ghetto-like immigrant clusters in Brooklyn and the Bronx. She was still worried that a "refugee complex" could damage Paul's confidence and limit his integration into America.

Getting Paul into college took three tries: First, Uncle Siegmund Singer in Oklahoma, the successful business owner who had supplied the affidavit only after assurance that she wouldn't ask for money, answered her query to say that Paul should not indulge in school when he should be working to support his dear old mother. How little he understood her. Next, Irma located a B'nai B'rith scholarship through her Hadassah connections and Paul left for Indiana University, only to complain that he was unhappy there. Irma couldn't tolerate the idea of putting Paul through another ordeal at school, and told him to pack his bags and come home. Finally, Irma tapped a friend of Erwin Kolmar's who knew the president of Queens College, who accepted Paul and made it possible for him to live at home.

"Mrs. Ehrlich has helped us considerably in raising funds for the transference of refugee children to Palestine," wrote Rebecca Sieff, chair of the Women's International Zionist Organization in her recommendation letter from London. "Her unbounded sincerity, charm, and intelligence are great assets."

But to Irma's deep disappointment, the apparent offer of a salaried position at Hadassah did not materialize into the full-time job she wanted. Few understood that she needed a career and was not someone who could donate her time to good works. She befriended Zionist influentials like Rabbi Stephen Wise, who had known of Jakob, and picked up a busy schedule of speaking assignments for Hadassah, the United Jewish Appeal, and similar organizations. It was a scramble at first. She had to travel to anywhere she was sent, bear up to constant publicity, and sustain her charisma into the evenings as a houseguest among wealthy supporters. I imagine her in Philadelphia in the sumptuous home of a department store magnate. "Vladivostok," she would muse. "That's where my brother-in-law was imprisoned for four years during the Great War ..." as her host family yielded to her storytelling voice. No wonder she had no trouble entertaining half a dozen guests at my parents' dinner table.

The woman who had once typed Jakob's speeches became an emissary from the birthplace of Zionism, an expert on the challenges of refugees from Nazi Europe, and a voice for children resettling in Palestine. Accolades poured in. "We thank you for waking us out of our quiet niche to the constructive work we can do," wrote one woman. "You have probably learned of how deeply your words penetrated our hearts, and the immediate response of many who heretofore had never been aroused to action," wrote another. Her ability *to make one feel*, as Vera Weizmann had said, moved people to donate. Their warmth kindled her sense of mission. Time after time, acquaintances became friends. Of one assignment she wrote:

I

I recall a beautiful day in June 1941. I traveled by bus and enjoyed the ride through the mountains. All I knew was that Grossinger's was the most renowned, most expensive resort hotel in the Catskills. Its hostess was famous for having built it from scratch after emigrating from Poland with her family. Mrs. Grossinger wanted to interest Hadassah members in Youth Aliyah [funding for displaced children in Palestine].

The meeting took place in the hotel dining room in the afternoon. The women were seated at tables with tea, coffee, and pastries. Mrs. Grossinger sat next to me on the platform and introduced me. In the middle of my talk a big piece of plaster fell from the ceiling to the table. The women jumped up screaming. I kept on talking, and they calmed down and sat down again. The meeting ended in harmony and was a success. Jennie Grossinger thanked me profusely for having saved the affair and invited me to be her guest in her house for the weekend. It was the beginning of a friendship that lasted until her death.

In the following years I used to meet Jennie at eight a.m. for breakfast at the Waldorf-Astoria when she was in New York. Twice I accepted her invitation as her private guest to a Yom Kippur service with one of the great cantors. She sent her Cadillac to pick me up.

I had assumed I would be lost in the great city, but my social contacts grew by leaps and bounds. Some came from the circles of my work. At the same time, friends and acquaintances arrived from Europe in ever-increasing numbers. One day, walking on Broadway, I ran into Fred Ehrlich, Jakob's nephew, and Berthold Hirsch, his niece Grete's husband. Both had made it from Europe, Berthold with his family after hair-raising risks and a narrow escape via France and Belgium. Fred was freed from a Gestapo prison on the German border by a Nazi with whom he had made friends in Siberia, where both had been prisoners of war. Fred was the first to reach New York and started a doll factory. He helped Berthold and one of his brothers to start one too. They succeeded after much effort.

Short assignments led to long ones when the Women's International Zionist Organization in London sent Irma on more months-long tours of Canada. In meetings with government officials she advocated passionately for larger immigration quotas to meet the European crisis. Traveling by railway, she visited the Maritime Provinces, saw the great interior from plush suites, and ventured to tiny Jewish enclaves in unlikely spots like Churchill in Manitoba and Medicine Hat in Alberta. Sometimes audience numbers exceeded one thousand.

Exhausting as her schedule could be, it was also exhilarating. She felt confident in the value of her work and found it fascinating.

2

I became familiar with sections and cross sections, currents and countercurrents within the Jewish communities. Very often I heard Yiddish spoken, which previously I had only read in books. My new experiences and challenges were of great help for my own survival, for as in England, I always felt lonely grieving for Jakob, asking myself what he would have said at each step. How wonderful and exciting it all would have been for him.

My extensive travels in England, Canada, and the US widened my views of the countries and peoples. I always had first-rate accommodations on trains and ships, no planes at that time. I met many people of different classes and due to my work learned a lot about the structure of the Jewish communities and their history in these lands.

I had grown up in an assimilated environment before National Socialism. I felt I was one of the people I lived among, as my family had done for centuries. I had read about but never seen Jewish refugees until the First World War, when I saw them receiving food at the railway platform in Plzeň during their flight from Russia's invasion of Austria's eastern provinces [Bukovina, Galicia].

In England there had been a strong influx from Eastern Europe, after pogroms and increasing anti-Semitism in Lithuania, the Ukraine, and Russia at the end of the nineteenth century. In Canada most of the Jewish communities consisted of descendants of Jews from Galicia, or as they would say, "Austria." Most of them were well-adjusted, many in leading positions financially and intellectually.

After we found a permanent home in Kew Gardens and my speaking engagements increased, I gained insight into the structure of Jewish life in the US. The first Jewish settlers came in the early nineteenth century from Central Europe, mostly Germany, and their descendants were in high finance, business, and all the higher walks of life. They were a class unto themselves, did not speak Yiddish, and did not welcome the masses driven by pogroms like the one in Kishinev in 1905.

Most of the Eastern European newcomers settled in Brooklyn, the Lower East Side, and the Bronx. They worked long hours in sweatshops and learned English painfully in evening classes. The second generation produced brilliant scholars, writers, artists, men of law and medicine, who remained guardians of the old traditions and taught their children Yiddish as well as English. Many of the brilliant Hadassah women I met were of that origin.

....

From the moment Irma and Paul landed in America, Europe fell ever deeper into crisis. The British Expeditionary Force barely escaped annihilation as it was evacuated from Europe at Dunkirk, and Paris fell to the Germans in June 1940, just three months after Irma and Paul left London. Stories about German atrocities circulated, but even Jews could not foresee the genocide that was taking shape. Later the world would learn that Nazis had made the decision in October 1941 to deport all Jews to camps to work and die, with Adolf Eichmann officiating. After a few experiments, they secretly began to install cyanide gas chambers at Auschwitz in a new extermination model that they would repeat in other designated death camps.

America's entry into the war brought more worry. She warned Paul not to "succumb to influences too far to the left, which was dangerous for newcomers." Would suspicion of communist leanings fall upon her foreign-born son? Would she be able to keep Paul out of war if a conscription system came into effect? Memories of Erwin and Jakob and the danger her family faced in Europe made the thought intolerable.

3

After Pearl Harbor [December 1941] the separation from Europe became complete. My parents, sister Edna and Fritz Werner, so many relatives and close friends, were trapped. I was gripped by fears. The daily news brought reports of ever-increasing, previously unimaginable inhumanities in the concentration camps.

Shortly after the US joined the war I received a letter from Jakob's nephew Hugo Deutsch. After the permit for Palestine I had obtained was sold by Rothenberg in Vienna, I had managed to get him an affidavit for the US. He had reached his time for a visa and happily informed me that he would be coming to New York. The next letter brought the shattering news that when he got to the American embassy to pick up the affidavit, it was closed for the first time. I never heard from him again.

For my parents and the Werners, I had arranged affidavits from Fred Ehrlich and friends who had factories in New York. The war made all my efforts futile. I received censored letters from them with ever-changing addresses, until they stopped altogether.

For a time I had some hope. The Nazis published propaganda reports of a model concentration camp in Theresienstadt, where the Jews of Prague and Holland were being deported. It was free for inspection by the Red Cross and any authorized international commission. I knew Theresienstadt, Terezín, as the garrison where my uncle General Alfred von Ptak had been commander years ago. My parents [Johann, 80, and Karla, 73] and Edna [sister, 48] were there. [From Terezín under censorship: Dearest Irmy and Pauli, best wishes, we're fine, hope you are too, kiss the Springarns for us, Love, Karla and Hans.] Time went by, I kept busy, but there was no news from Theresienstadt. I knew from Sofie Löwenherz that Erna Patak and Rabbi Murmelstein were there as leaders who had contact with the Gestapo, which gave me hope that they would protect my family.

In March 1943 I received a censored postal card from Rudi Brok [son of Irma's sister Mela] from a labor camp near Warsaw. In April there was an uprising by inmates and liquidation of the Warsaw ghetto. I never heard from Rudi again.

As the war dragged on, the threat of the draft became one of my greatest heartaches. I had a meeting in Washington that was of great importance. The widow of Justice Brandeis and wife of Justice Frankfurter had made it known they would attend. I arrived the day before and was the guest of the president of the Hadassah chapter. She was most gracious and took me sightseeing to Mount Vernon and the National Gallery, and to lunch with members of the organization. When we returned to her house in the afternoon for a rest, she brought the evening paper to my room. There was the bold headline: The Senate had voted to require all young men to register for the draft. [December 20, 1942. The draft was selective before then and college deferments were still being allowed.] I had a stabbing pain and felt completely lost. I wonder how I found the composure to face exacting publicity that evening.

Paul finished his college degree [Queens College, chemistry, 1944], and I hoped officer training would delay him but was rudely awakened when somebody told me this was not the time for such fancy projects. The summer of 1944 was a time of suspense. Paul's basic training was drawing to a close. I had hoped the war would end soon after the invasion [D-Day, June 6, 1944], but fierce fighting was ongoing. In July, news of the attempted assassination of Hitler came during a weekend with friends in Long Island. We waited hopefully. Hitler, though shaken, got away with his life. Paul wrote one day that he was scheduled to be shipped overseas.

On August 27, 1944, Paul came to see me. It was a beautiful day. We strolled in Forest Park and lay in the sun at the point where one can see the ocean. We had dinner and took the subway to Rockefeller Center for the last show. It was Pearl Buck's *The Good Earth*. As we were winding up the stairs in line we passed by high mirrors on the walls. Paul looked so tall next to me, so handsome in his uniform. My heart ached. After some time he looked at his wristwatch. It was midnight. He stood up, kissed me, said, "Happy Birthday, Mother," and left. For a while I could not move. It had been the farewell. Then I took the subway back to Kew Gardens alone.

....

Paul had enlisted after college in spite of his mother's anguish and wrote obscure cultural references into notes home to reassure her and fool the censors. Irma said she was "elated when Paul wrote he had gone hunting with natives, sighted a hare, scared a cow, and caught a cold. That meant, of course, Belgium and the Ardennes." Fortunately, Paul was not in his original unit when they suffered severe casualties during the Battle of the Bulge. Because of his scientific and German language skills, he was sent with the joint US–British T-Force to secure German scientific equipment at industrial sites before it could be looted or destroyed by retreating Germans or advancing Russians. T-Force programs would eventually capture brilliant scientists like German rocket engineer Wernher von Braun, who later helped to launch America's space program.

Irma agonized over his safety until the long war in Europe ended in May 1945. She tried to be home each day at ten a.m. to check for mail from him before taking the F train into the city. Kind friends distracted her with invitations to weekend coffee hours and dinners. Viennese émigrés who had arrived years earlier took her to the Frick museum and the Russian Tea Room, and shared their season tickets to Carnegie Hall performances.

Between appointments in midtown Manhattan on June 29, 1945, Irma watched from the steps of St. Paul's cathedral as General Eisenhower paraded by under a litter of ticker tape. As concentration camps were liberated, organizations like the Red Cross helped Irma to learn the unthinkable extent of her family losses. She traced her parents, sister and brother-in-law, cousins, school friends whose lives ended in those terrible years in Europe, 1942–1944 (see Afterword). A lawyer named Dr. Armand Eisler, who had been with Jakob in Dachau, found her and told her the truth. He had indeed died of a heart attack, as she was told, but only after severe beatings by a guard during forced labor. Irma commissioned a stone of Swedish granite to be placed on his grave.

Paul Ehrlich came home a bona fide American guy telling only the tales that made the army seem like comic opera. He studied for his PhD in chemistry under the GI Bill at the University of Wisconsin at Madison, where he met a long-stemmed blond and blue-eyed girl named Celia Lesley, just in time for the baby boom. Boom, Daniel Jakob; boom, James Leonard; boom, Catherine (that's me); boom, Margot; boom, Paul Roger.

....

Irma rebuilt a network of friends in New York, many of whom shared a past in Europe. She joined them for weekends at their staffed Hudson Valley homes and Long Island beach houses, walked with them along Jones Beach, and met them in the city for concerts. New arrivals like the Löwenherzes, who ended up living two blocks away, relied on family and friends to get back on their feet.

With the end of the war, Britain asked the United Nations to take up the question of how to transition the British Mandate in Palestine into an independent state. In the wake of the Holocaust, the need for a Jewish homeland had become clear. Irma watched as United Nations recommendations led to the State of Israel in 1948, and swelled with pride when Chaim Weizmann, the man who tried to hire her as his personal secretary in London, was elected as Israel's first president in 1949.

Irma had one more job transition in store. Her work as an immigration advocate and emergency fundraiser for displaced children declined with peacetime and the founding of Israel. Irma took up steady work as a paralegal secretary in the law office of Miller & Haim in Midtown Manhattan, where her knowledge of shorthand, European languages, and legal process was useful. Irma prepared survivor claims for reparations from Germany. She interviewed refugees and concentration camp survivors in the European language of their choice, immersing herself in the traumas they had suffered and documenting each detail of their losses to submit in claims to the German government. Yet she remained ineligible for benefits because Austria was posing as "Hitler's first victim" and refusing to compensate for stolen lives and possessions as though the embrace of Nazi rule had never happened.

Irma was poorly paid as a woman and non-lawyer in the office, and the work could be grueling. Client stories burnt traumatic images of her parents' last months into her mind. Yet her careful listening restored fortunes and brought up names and connections that helped to unite friends and family, healing her as it healed them. When reparation eligibility rules broadened, Irma refreshed her clients' applications. Attending one by one to the wronged, Irma dignified their experiences and her own, restored equilibrium, made life more meaningful. Irma's pride ripened into a warm compassion that reached out to repair the world.

Law partners at Miller & Haim registered legal claims in terms of material loss and physical injury only, in accordance with their training. Steeped in Freud from her years in Vienna, Irma ignored that legal precedent and let her heart speak. "Bad dreams," her case histories listed, even though no country paid out for psychological injury. Legally significant or not, Irma's documents bore witness to the truth.

Over the years, Miller & Haim lawyers thought reparations had played out and turned the seemingly worthless files over to Irma as the only one who wanted to maintain pursuit. Her persistence paid off. German courts ultimately acknowledged what we now call post-traumatic stress disorder (PTSD) as an injury. They began paying compensation for trauma suffered under Nazi hands *if the original claims recorded the injuries.* Irma's stubborn insistence on documenting trauma as "bad dreams" was the basis for a new set of claims that she filed and won. Legal fees for her clients' belated compensation brought Irma a financial windfall to honor a moral triumph.

Clients showed their appreciation over many years. I commented on her elegant Italian double-knit suit in emerald green, with bordered jacket and pencil skirt. "I got it," she said, meaning it was a gift from a grateful client in the garment business. I recall the impossibly soft pink cashmere bathrobe her grandchildren snuggled into during holiday visits, a thank-you from either the B. Altman & Company department store family or the textile merchant Altmann family she had known in Vienna. One day, her jet-beaded black wool jacket from an appreciative supporter

in Winnipeg would be mine. As Paul and Celia raised five children on a professor's salary, Irma chipped in with extras like a
grandson's school fees and my round-trip airline tickets to Japan.

....

From her old-world sanctuary in New York, Irma watched the
news as Adolf Eichmann sat unrepentantly through his trial in
Jerusalem for war crimes and was hanged in Israel in 1962. After
haunting Jakob's funeral and Irma's exit with reptilian eye, Eichmann had overseen the brutal roundup and transport by locked
boxcar of whole communities to certain death. At the end of the
war he escaped to Argentina with the assistance of an organized
network of collaborators and lived as Ricardo Klement, a sales-
man, until hunted, drugged, and abducted in a coffin by Israeli
commandos who offered him up for judgment years after other
Nazis were tried and hanged at Nuremberg.

In 1964, at the age of seventy-four, Irma traveled to Israel
to see the country that Jakob and she had helped to realize, a
land full of people that she and Jakob had saved through their
interventions. Irma climbed Mount Zion among pilgrims in
traditional dress, feeling she had stepped into an illustrated
Bible, and heard Hebrew songs sung by a robust new generation of Israelis. I think she believed that Jews and Arabs would
bridge their differences over time. Fragrance wafting from trees
recalled her grandparents' booklets bound in Lebanese cedar, sent
in appreciation for their donations to poor Jewish settlements
in Palestine long ago. Among the chiseled stones of the ruined
temple, at the Wailing Wall, Irma cried for Jakob, her parents,
her sister, and too many more.

Irma celebrated Passover with her family members on Mount
Carmel in Haifa: Hannah Werner Braun, the niece she had rescued via the Kindertransport, and her family; and cousins Paul
and Ernst Singer, who had swum ashore after their transport

vessel, the *Patria*, was sunk. Together they recited the story of Jewish perseverance and felt the joy of ritual reunion.

Her next big trip came in 1971 when she flew to Japan to visit me, the granddaughter she had inspired to learn languages as my passport to a wider world.

*Paul Ehrlich made good on his access to the
American PX by bartering high-value cigarettes for a fine violin.*

Paul and I

After leaving Japan in 1972 I went straight to Ann Arbor to study Asian languages at the University of Michigan. One day I came home to my four-woman apartment and roommate Susan's message: "A man with an accent called for you. He didn't leave a message. He said he'd call back."

Who could that be? I wondered. I wasn't dating any foreign man and couldn't even think of one who might have my phone number.

"I think it was your father," Susan said. My father didn't have an accent. I was mystified until Papa called back wanting to know what my mother would want for Christmas. Sure, he pronounced the second "l" in Lincoln and a "w" occasionally veered into a "v." He had a few idiosyncrasies but hardly a German accent, I thought. Such traces of Viennese origins reside unconsciously in my being.

My college crowd included students from nearby Bloomfield Hills and suburban New York who used words like *oy vey* and *schmuck* and *tchotchke* playfully. I knew what they meant because I had read Leo Rosten's hilarious *The Joys of Yiddish*. My Jewish friends spoofed guilt-tripping relatives, imitated their funny shrugs, and even held an off-key Seder—my first Seder of any kind. Those things never came up in rural Massachusetts, where I recall kids polling fellow students on the school bus. "How many Catholics? How many Protestants?" Tallies taken and forgotten, the poll was complete. Until college, I was unaware that Jewish enclaves were a living cultural phenomenon outside of New York City.

My home had always included faint Austrian accents. Mozart was our musical mascot, the composer Papa practiced most often for his amateur string quartet. In adulthood I learned that the ditty he played to warm up on his violin was the musical call of the streetcar conductor on Vienna's Hütteldorf line, not Mozart at all. Coffee could be prepared *mit oder ohne mit,* that is, *with or "without-with"* whipped cream, a jaunty phrase suggesting the Viennese love for cream. My siblings and I knew some phrases in German, never Yiddish, as that was not in Irma or Paul's culture. We picked up refrains from Papa's vinyl recordings of sentimental Viennese drinking songs in a local Viennese dialect that twists vowels, swallows syllables, and sounds dopey-drunken to the high-German speaker. The whole family knew about the day the angels got leave from God to descend for a drinking spree in Vienna and crowded the #38 streetcar heading to the wine district of Grinzing. In Viennese, a #38 car was a sloppy *achtadress'ger Wagn* rather than a proper *achtundreissiger Wagen,* and good was *guat* rather than *gut.* Papa liked to deploy choice bits of dialect in Irma's hearing to make her hair stand on end.

Paul had taken to America like a golden retriever to water. "An American is someone who lives in America," he liked to say, loving the egalitarian and meritocratic feel relative to authoritarian Austria and tradition-bound England. In Austria he'd been "arrested" at age six in Türkenschanz Park for stepping off the sidewalk to pick up a fallen chestnut. Irma had to appease the police by reporting remorse for this crime. Under Hitler's militant fascism, Paul's childhood came to an abrupt end. In England, class and custom meant boys of modest ability could nonetheless lord it over him as an immigrant. Papa ridiculed entitled, regimented, and officious behavior ever after.

....

Paul pursued a long career in chemistry as a researcher and a professor at the State University of New York at Buffalo. He liked the rationality of science in contrast to the irrational politics that had claimed his father. Paul elevated "intellectual" to high praise, an egghead label his kids had to live up to at home but live down in the public school system. Baseball and football came too late in his life for him to teach them to us; instead, we bonded while hiking. Peanut butter wasn't food. He had no idea that barbecuing was an American man's civic duty. These were the Austrian accents we knew about, unlike the ones in his speech. Our mother let us join the Cub Scouts and Brownies, but Papa mocked us as willing little Brownshirts in uniform.

My parents were in full agreement on the sacred qualities of music, mountains, and education. Hiking was good. I got so many "attagirls" from Papa that I hiked Mount Washington unaided at the age of four. Skiing was good. I was *schussing* down the slope of our apple orchard on wooden skis by the age of five, and then on to Stowe and Breadloaf ski resorts. Classical music was good. I didn't dare play the Beatles at home for fear of scorn. We all accepted that organized religion was human but hiking divine, that intelligence was innate but achievement was earned, that music is a form of love.

My creative mother, the California-raised daughter of Anglo-American nominally Christian parents, coined the adjective *ehrlich* to encompass this set of values. In fact, *ehrlich* means honest, as in forthright, and turns up a maddening cascade of "honestly, truly, really" miscues in a German Google search for family.

Irma visited three times a year, at Christmas, Easter, and some part of the summer that included a trip to the mountains.

When she recounted sagas about German clients and Austrian emigrants, Paul's mind went into orbit and a vacancy came across his face. "Absent-minded professor thinking about entropy," we teased, but he was absent with intent.

By airborne transmission, I got the impression that Jewish holidays were about reliving tragedy and Jewish affairs meant a mournful fixation on the Holocaust. Paul wasn't exactly evasive about that part of his past, but he wasn't interested in dwelling there. He was not going to let Jewishness define his future or ours. With our mixed parentage and the Jewish practice of assigning religious heritage from the maternal side, my siblings and I were neither Austrian Americans nor Jewish Americans.

We learned from Irma and Paul that Austria had "welcomed Hitler with open arms," and saw Kurt Waldheim, an ex-Nazi, hold power in the 1980s. Meanwhile, Paul cracked up over a *Mad* magazine satire of *The Sound of Music* in which a useless high-ranking officer declares, "I have a full day of hanging around to do!" Hollywood brought us *Sophie's Choice* and *Schindler's List* and ever more realistic accounts of concentration camps and vicious neighbor-on-neighbor violence. I wondered whether Paul was *too* forgiving of Austria, the place that betrayed his family. Paul seemed to think that the national character of Austria was less vicious than hedonistic, and casually willing to sing along to any tune. Irma agreed, remembering the Viennese persona as playful, superficial, and flirtatious but not serious. This was summed up in the refrain *"Glücklich ist wer vergisst was doch nicht zu ändern ist,"* from *Die Fledermaus,* an operetta composed by Johann Strauss II to a libretto by Karl Haffner and Richard Genée: *Happy are they who ignore what they cannot change.*

Another of Papa's favorite songs shows that even German rocket scientists may ignore what they can't change. "Wernher von Braun," composed and sung by fellow scientist Tom Lehrer, evokes the captured German rocket scientist who switched sides after Germany lost the war.

Gather 'round while I sing you of Wernher von Braun,
A man whose allegiance is ruled by expedience.
Call him a Nazi, he won't even frown,
"Ha, Nazi, Schmazi," says Wernher von Braun.

Don't say that he's hypocritical,
Say rather that he's apolitical.
"Once the rockets are up, who cares where they come down?
That's not my department," says Wernher von Braun.

Only now as I think it through do I see how Paul avoided being oppressed by the anger I felt on his behalf toward Vienna. Irma had body-blocked him from taking on "a refugee complex" of otherness and loss. She showed by example that it does not serve to live as a victim with a grudge, too proud to move on, as if owed some unpayable debt from the past. The US Army's victory, his sociable nature, and his feeling of welcome here did the rest.

Paul became a naturalized American citizen in Jacksonville, Florida, in 1944 as prelude to shipping out as a soldier. He was fortunate that the war had less than a year to go, and that he was seconded into the T-Force before his unit suffered badly in the Battle of the Bulge. The job of the T-Force was to claim German scientific and industrial equipment of value, so Paul's knowledge of German helped to save him from one of the worst battles in the war. Just days after German surrender in Berlin and Hitler's suicide on April 30, 1945, Paul took part in a raid on a ship-building and armaments yard in Kiel, Germany. American troops succeeded in arriving before the Russians but faced a tense stand-off with armed German defenders before superior officers told them to stand down. Other T-Force operations captured leading scientists including Wernher von Braun, celebrated with cheeky humor in the song above, who went from designing missiles for Germany to seeding America's nuclear program.

After unconditional German surrender on May 7, 1945, Paul learned that demobilization could take up to a year. He signed on to do intelligence work out of a base in Friesen, Germany, and later served at Nuremberg interviewing Nazis in German as the court meted out twelve death sentences to those deemed most responsible. The Nazi official who was a particular bane to this family, Adolf Eichmann, would evade capture until 1960.

Paul and his US Army pals lived it up as conquering heroes in Europe. Mountains and music figured largely, as did young women overjoyed by the war's end. American GIs had access to the PX for rations and cigarettes, which were excellent for gifts and barter. Paul traded several cartons of cigarettes for the beautiful violin he played for the rest of his life. In October 1945 his commanding officer was asked to supply a US Army Jeep and driver to take a colonel to Vienna. He assigned the job to Paul, despite having to forge a military driver's license for him. Six feet tall, chiseled and fit in pressed GI khakis, Paul drove triumphantly into Vienna eight years after his expulsion. He wrote home to his mother:

October 22, 1945
Dear Mutti,
Excuse the long silence. You will if I tell you why. Guess where I was. Yes, in Vienna. In spite of the destruction, it still is very much the old Vienna. It differs vastly from the cities in Germany. Everything is shot up in Germany; life has an air of utter unreality. Vienna appears entirely normal. Much the same way it was in 1938. People walk around, still hungry, although not quite as badly as a month ago, but well-dressed.

It's hard to describe my feelings. Vienna is still a beautiful city, it has style, but you somehow have the feeling that it keeps harping on a tune that has been played over so many times that nobody believes it anymore.

The only thing which affected me strongly was the Mazuras [Paul's nanny, Rosa, and her husband, Sylvester, who lived in the ground-floor apartment of the building where the Ehrlichs had lived]. It was all as touching as you can imagine. They were both thin and appear shrunk up, but both are lively and seem in good health. I wish I could find time to write about all the details, the way they kissed me on the street, the incendiary bomb which made a tiny hole in the roof and no other damage, etc. It all seemed so natural, as though continuing a conversation you had had the night before—all of Vienna seemed that way. It was terrible to say goodbye.

The grave [Jakob's] is in excellent shape, lots of stones, and I put a beautiful wreath of roses on it. Rosa and Sylvester were preparing to go there for All Saints' Day.

You do know, don't you (this comes via Erna Patak and Rosa Mazura), that both grandparents are dead. There is no news on the Werners [Irma's sister and her husband].

The Burgtheater (open in the Ronacher) and the Opera are burnt out but are being repaired, and the Stephansdom isn't irreparable either. The Parliament and the Rathaus are undamaged, and the city picture as a whole hasn't suffered too much. Every single theater that played in 1938 plays today. Political parties hold their meetings and the notice boards are full.

I may go to school at the Sorbonne for two months beginning next week. And thus I amble from one pleasure into another. No word at all from you.
Paul

I recall Irma saying she would never go back to Vienna. But she went in 1974, the year Paul took a sabbatical at Oxford University with my younger siblings in tow. Irma took it as a chance to visit Jakob's grave with family and see the marble block she had commissioned from abroad—laid horizontally lest Nazis knock over a standing stone.

A brother and I joined our parents on subsequent trips to Vienna, and on a 2007 trip to London we called on MP Greville Janner, who had been ten years old when his parents welcomed Irma and Paul into their home in 1938. He took us to the House of Lords, where his eccentric mannerisms made us wonder whether he was altogether okay. My husband and I hiked flower-strewn meadows from an Alpine lodge with my parents, heard the angelic voices of the Vienna Boys' Choir at the lofty Hofburg Chapel, indulged at Café Central, and walked from 22 Weimarerstrasse through the old neighborhood where Paul pointed out the homes of his old school pals.

Paul was seventy-five years old in 1999 when he flew to Vienna for a capping reconciliation with the past. A leader at Paul's old school, Döblinger Gymnasium 19, had assigned history students to investigate what happened to the Jewish students expelled by Nazi order on April 29, 1938. Paul counted it a brave reckoning by the teacher, Martin Krist, and participated by flying in for the school's presentation. Some of the attending survivors, overwhelmed by psychological damage, found no solace at the event. Scientist and teacher Paul was able to embrace the young generation's willingness to learn history by looking at its impact on individuals. He told them that his experience was quite unlike that of his mother, who suffered the loss of most of her family:

> A middle-school student is not tied to the past, and can form a new worldview without difficulty—one hardly has a worldview at fifteen—and the change is particularly easy in the USA. You can unreservedly see yourself as an American wherever you were born, especially if you are very young and have experienced fascism.

Paul wanted to acknowledge the school's initiative. He and a few others contributed to a small library fund and put a scientific spin on their purpose. Paul wrote: "In appreciation of Martin Krist and the students who uncovered a part of history brought about by the brutal use of pseudoscience, this fund is dedicated to the pursuit of studies that illuminate the nature of true science and its ethical consequences." I thought a donation was going a bit far, but the young students' honesty touched his generous heart. Facing the truth would keep fascism in retreat, they thought.

Paul and Irma imprinted on all of his children: I took to languages, my sister to music. Two brothers followed in science, and one is a civil liberties activist. We all knew that hiking with Papa was the best way to connect with him. His advice usually came down to a bemused observation like Yogi Berra's "When you come to a fork in the road, take it," followed by "I don't think you can go wrong," which was reassurance enough. All of us got the hiking gene, and seek enlightenment, inspiration, humility, and truth by gazing upward at holy tree canopies and striding freely under open skies.

"What was Jakob like?" I asked Paul as we strolled the hills outside Vienna where his family had spent Sundays. I imagined that Jakob, with his important professional responsibilities, was a bit of a disciplinarian at home. But that was not so. "He was emotionally available," Paul said, using a modern lingo that hits home: it is precisely what I say about Paul.

Karla Singer Hütter wore diamond earrings, 1888 and about 1920

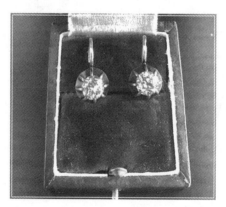

Karla's earrings, rediscovered.

Appraisal

My earliest memories of Irma come from Christmas mornings in our rural Massachusetts home, when she—rosy-cheeked, snowy-haired, and merry as Santa Claus—led a line of grandchildren past the twinkling tree to the mantle and back into our bedrooms, where we plundered our stockings before our parents arose. Gifts she brought from FAO Schwarz and B. Altman in Manhattan would appear, and hard candies as colorful as kaleidoscopes. Beautiful books from Scribner's illustrated Grandma's former land of fairy tales and castles, where her Jewish mother once decorated the family tree. A Christmas tree was a shared cultural symbol in the Germanic tradition, and not in conflict with a Hanukkah celebration Irma might attend in New York.

....

I grew up without a specific religious imprint and with good reason to think it is safer not to be Jewish. My four siblings and

I were no less Christian than we were Jewish by parental heritage, and both seemed fraught to me—manipulative, aggrandizing, and divisive in practice, whatever virtues they might have. And so I was surprised when my father lit candles on Irma's eagle-topped silver menorah at her passing in December of 1986. I thought I was seeing him honor Jewish tradition for the first time. (He knew that a *Jahrzeit* candle would have been more appropriate, but the menorah symbolized Irma for his family.) I was taken aback in a much later conversation when his Jewish roots surfaced. We were hiking along a ridge in the White Mountains when I asked him, "Which historical figure do you most admire?"

"Well, Cat. I'd have to say Moses," he said.

"Moses? Why?" I asked.

"Because he led his people to the Promised Land."

How humbling, I thought, for Paul to have two parents who led thousands to sanctuary in the Promised Land of Israel. Sure enough, traces of his Jewish upbringing remained. My own reading was that Paul led his mother to the secular Promised Land, when at sixteen he chose to brave a new start in America—and so he was Moses to me.

....

Imprints of heritage live hidden or expressed, recessive or dominant, in our hybrid selves. Adaptation is our family tradition. Irma accepted Paul's choice to drop overt religious observance and become American. Yet he yodeled in the mountains as if by instinct, like a beagle baying at the moon. A heart has home for many facets of identity.

National borders change or close; we need new passports to come and go. Meanwhile, languages surmount barriers that passports cannot scale. German, French, and English, spoken just so, carried Irma across. In Vienna when Gestapo agents seized Irma's passport, she used German to coax a rabid Nazi to expedite a key document. Only then, after Eichmann extorted sufficient funds, did he issue the one-way kick out the door that passed as a passport. Stuck at the Channel as war broke out, stateless and passport-less, Irma spoke in perfect French to the *gentil* boat captain who agreed to ferry her across to safety. Speaking in English so expressively that people *felt* what she said, Irma helped the European Jewish diaspora pass to new homelands, earn new passports, and regenerate their lives.

Irma's virtual passport of language became mine. I wanted to explore the world and so I studied languages. Learning Japanese earned me a first passport, a fascinating first year abroad, and a first sense of how it feels to live as a racial minority or "other." In graduate school studying for a diplomatic career, I thought how Irma might have been a diplomat in a later era, like Madeleine Albright. When I redirected my career plan to international business, it was important to overcome my fear of public speaking. I summoned my inner Irma for courage as I addressed audiences in Chinese in Beijing, Japanese in Tokyo, and English in America.

I think back to the time when I was seventeen in Japan, when I still thought of Irma as battle-scarred but victorious. Life was not suffering, I thought, and believed she agreed. It took the Buddhist priest Hata's query about reincarnation—would she choose to live again—and Irma's shocking answer, "no," to make me see that Irma was not simply stoic, and that her suffering was not just a thing of the past. How naive I was, to have absorbed only the righteousness and not the trauma. Yet there, perhaps, was her greatest victory—she wanted us to feel free to adapt, and not bear her suffering across generations.

Compassion eases suffering, pundits say. It reaches out to pain and redirects it toward purpose. Irma carried herself and Paul through dark times by radiating compassion that restored many. Her compassion emerged from pride under pressure, I think, like diamonds from carbon. Like the diamond earrings that persevered through lifetimes to shine new light on old family bonds for me.

My father, Paul, died suddenly in 2003 at the age of seventy-nine. Grieving in his office, I looked into a small leather box resting in his solid oak desk drawer and found a pair of crystalline buds set on silver ear loops, stowed like dormant links to the past. Where did they come from? Could they be diamonds?

A few weeks later an appraiser clapped a jeweler's loupe to his eye and told me they were indeed diamonds set in silver, stamped "Austria," the style dating from about 1860. "Get them insured," he said, "and wear them." Rushing home to compare a family photo, I zoomed in on Karla Hütter, Irma's mother, and I knew. These came from the Imperial and Royal Jewelers on Stephansplatz in Vienna, the shop owned by Karla's uncle Lippmann Kohner.

This means, I know from Irma's pages, that Karla kept back a few precious pieces when she sold her other jewelry to save the family business in 1896. Could they have belonged to her mother, Julia, before her? Perhaps. The photos are inconclusive. But I know why they did not become Nazi loot. My great-grandmother Karla smuggled them over a rope into Irma's hand at their last goodbye at Prague airport in September 1938. Of the eleven people on Karla's side of the rope, nine died in the Holocaust. Yet Karla's form of insurance, Karla's currency of love, crossed over the line dividing premature death and life. Those diamonds link generations of women who passed along facets of themselves—their courage, their stories, their indestructible sparkle—to me.

Austria has continued to reckon with the years that scarred Irma's and Paul's generations. After Paul's restorative visit to his Vienna high school in 1999, new reparation offers brought us $6,000 for home and office leases, but nothing for stolen property, savings, prison murder, and trauma. Nothing for the "bad dreams" Irma documented for others, and so helped to establish as legal precedent for trauma compensation. But Irma had already taught us not to live for unpayable debts. Her gems of inheritance, diamonds and memoir pages alike, mean more than any form of reparations.

Paul was heartened to see a plaque honoring Jakob and other murdered Jewish leaders mounted at Vienna's City Hall. In 2012, a brass plate of remembrance (*Stolperstein*) was embedded outside Jakob Ehrlich's last home at 22 Weimarer Street. Children and grandchildren of those wrongfully expelled in 1938 are now eligible for Austrian citizenship. Dual citizenship, an adaptation that anti-Zionist German nationalists of yore would have attacked as "having two fatherlands," has become fashionable.

Irma worked until the age of eighty-six to repair the world, then retired to an apartment near my parents' house in Buffalo, New York. She served caviar when I came to tea. Her white hair grew feathery, like a dandelion puff blowing apart, as she embodied nearly a century of history. I flew in from Hong Kong to her bedside before she let go at ninety-six, and felt her parting hand pass something intangible to me for safekeeping, that I might pass it on to you.

Notable Names

Irma intersected with a many prominent people in her life in brief or pivotal ways. Here I list some of the public figures in her network, followed by a few words about family and friends. May Irma's karmic connections keep rolling via this book.

Public Figures

PRAGUE

Albert Einstein
1879–1955
Nobel Prize–winning theoretical physicist who became a full professor at the German Charles-Ferdinand University in Prague in 1911 while developing his theory of relativity. Einstein aided Zionist causes such as the Hebrew University in Jerusalem, opened in 1925. His presence in Prague while Irma was a student there speaks to the lively intellectual ferment she felt.

Franz Kafka
1883–1924
Literary giant whose fame grew after his friend and executor Max Brod published some of his works posthumously. He was a distant cousin to Irma and, though graduated, attended some lectures at Charles University while Irma was there.

VIENNA

Bernhard Altmann
1888–1960

Textile manufacturer who fled Vienna on the night of the Anschluss and saved his family from abroad. The book *The Lady in Gold* and the film *Woman in Gold* tell the story of his sister-in-law Maria Altmann's fight to recover the famous Klimt portrait of her aunt, confiscated and held by the Austrian government. Helen Mirren, who played Maria Altmann in the film, would make a terrific Irma, as would Meryl Streep. The Altmanns were friends of Jakob and Irma.

Rabbi Zwi Perez Chajes
1876–1927

Chief rabbi of Vienna's Jewish community from 1918–1927, and chair of the Zionist General Council of the World Zionist Organization from 1921–1925. He was a friend to Irma and Jakob.

Jakob Ehrlich
1877–1938

Lawyer, politician, and Zionist leader in Vienna's city council, Vienna's Jewish Community Organization, and the Austrian Zionist Federation; the first prominent Austrian to die at Dachau. He was Irma's husband and the author's grandfather.

Otto Adolf Eichmann
1906–1962

German-Austrian SS (*Schutzstaffel*) Nazi responsible for mass emigration of Jews from Austria and later mass deportations to extermination camps. He escaped to Argentina after the war but was captured by Nazi hunters in 1960, tried for war crimes in Jerusalem, and hanged in 1962. His ominous presence at both Jakob's funeral and Irma's release reflects his twisted agenda.

Desider Friedmann, and his wife, Ellie, a social connector
1880–1944
Member of the Austrian parliament, 1934–1938; Zionist leader of Vienna's Jewish community, 1933–1938; killed with his wife, Ellie, as part of the last transport from Terezín to Auschwitz. In 1990, a plaza not far from Café Central was renamed Desider-Friedmann-Platz. He was a colleague to Jakob; Ellie made critical connections for Irma in London.

Theodor Herzl
1860–1904
Austro-Hungarian journalist whose book *The Jewish State* catalyzed the Zionist movement; founder of the World Zionist Congresses, which led to the State of Israel. At Vienna's *New Free Press*, he helped to launch the career of literary author Stefan Zweig. He inspired Jakob Ehrlich at the University of Vienna.

Josef Löwenherz and his wife, Sofie, a social connector
1884–1946
Galician-born Zionist, lawyer, and administrative head of Vienna's Jewish community from 1936–1944. In serving under Eichmann, he expedited emigration of 125,000 Austrian Jews but faced impossible choices as Nazi policy turned to deportation and extermination. After the war he was tried by a Jewish tribunal (people's court) as a collaborator and acquitted. Josef was Jakob's younger colleague, and Irma saw them postwar in New York.

Benjamin Murmelstein
1905–1989
Controversial Austrian rabbi in Vienna who worked with Josef Löwenherz and others under Eichmann to expedite Jewish emigration. As an elder at Terezín, he triaged Jewish lives and earned bitter enemies. Irma's hope that he would protect her elderly parents there was unrealistic.

Erna Patak
1871–1955

Philanthropic Zionist activist who became the first president of the Austrian branch of the Women's International Zionist Organization. After liberation from Terezín, she rang the doorbell at her Vienna mansion and was met by the new owner, her family maid, who cried, "For heaven's sake, they didn't gas you?" She emigrated to Palestine, where her daughter had settled. She was a friend and matchmaker to Irma.

Kurt Schuschnigg
1897–1977

Chancellor of the Federal State of Austria from 1934–1938 who banned the Nazi party and appointed Jewish representatives to his cabinet but was cornered by Hitler and resigned. Jakob Ehrlich worked with him. Schuschnigg became a professor in St. Louis, Missouri, where Paul Ehrlich called on him in the 1960s in a salute to his failed "better German state."

LONDON

Sir Wyndham Deedes
1883–1956

Brigadier general and chief secretary to the British high commissioner of the British Mandate of Palestine. He secured a full scholarship for Paul to go to Brighton College.

Lady Violet Isaacs, Marchioness of Reading
1895–1973

Wealthy philanthropist, daughter of Zionist Alfred Mond, and daughter-in-law to the viceroy of India, Lord Reading. She exemplifies aristocratic noblesse oblige in Irma's British circles.

Barnett Janner and his wife, Elsie
1892–1982

Member of parliament from 1931–1935 and 1945–1970, knighted in 1961, and made a life peer in 1970. Leading Zionist. Elsie Janner, 1905–1994, was a magistrate and social worker who led many Jewish organizations and was awarded a CBE for public service. They gave sanctuary to Irma and Paul.

Greville Janner
1928–2015

Barrister, politician, and son of Barnett and Elsie. He was a British MP from 1970–1997, elevated to the House of Lords, and chair of the Board of Deputies of British Jews as recounted in his 2003 memoir, *To Life!* He welcomed Ehrlich descendants to the House of Lords. Accusations of child sexual abuse, which he and his family denied, dogged him late in life. His mother's counsel to Irma that British boarding schools were rife with sexual misconduct, but that it was "not British" for parents to intervene, seems poignant in retrospect.

Madame Dorothy de Rothschild
1895–1988

Noted philanthropist and wife of Liberal politician James de Rothschild, who actively supported Zionist causes. Her connections helped Irma to save lives.

Viscountess Beatrice Samuel
1871–1959

Suffragist and the wife of Sir Herbert Samuel, MP, Liberal party leader from 1931–1935, who was the first high commissioner of Mandate Palestine. She hosted the high society luncheon that signaled Irma's social acceptance in London.

Lady Rebecca Sieff
1890–1966

First president and a founder of the Women's International Zionist Organization. Her husband, Israel Sieff, was also a Zionist. She and her sisters Miriam Sacher and Lady Mathilda Marks were of Marks & Spencer department store lineage and philanthropists. She hosted an event in London for Irma and made connections for her in New York.

Celina Sokolow
1886 –1984

Polish-born physician, philanthropist, and daughter of Nahum Sokolow, who was secretary general of the World Zionist Organization. Irma was a guest speaker at her aristocratic home for fundraising events.

Chaim Weizmann and his wife, Vera
1874–1952

Biochemist, diplomat, visionary Zionist, and the first president of Israel in 1949. He came to prominence in Britain by discovering a bacterial fermentation process for acetone, used in explosives in World War I. He was president of the World Zionist Organization and a mentor to Jakob. For Paul's sake, Irma turned down the opportunity to become his personal secretary, which would have been a fascinating job.

Vera Weizmann
1881–1966

Pediatrician, president of the Women's International Zionist Organization, and president of Youth Aliyah in Israel. Her appreciation of Irma's talent *made* Irma's career.

United States

Justice Louis Brandeis
1856–1941
Associate justice on the Supreme Court of the United States from 1916 to 1939, social justice pioneer, and Zionist. Irma lobbied for refugees with his widow.

Justice Felix Frankfurter
1882–1965
Vienna-born associate justice of the Supreme Court of the United States from 1939 to 1962 and a founder of the American Civil Liberties Union (who supported the founding of a Jewish state). Irma lobbied for refugees with his wife.

Jennie Grossinger
1892–1972
Proprietress of the famous Grossinger's Catskill Resort Hotel, doyenne of the Borscht Belt set, and hostess to the rich and famous. Irma befriended her while raising funds for Youth Aliyah.

Rabbi Stephen Samuel Wise
1874–1949
American Reform rabbi and Zionist activist who, along with Justices Brandeis and Frankfurter, influenced American policy toward Jews during the administrations of presidents Woodrow Wilson and Franklin D. Roosevelt. He served as president of the Keren Hayesod building fund for Palestine and president of the American Jewish Congress, among other roles. He helped Irma to get her first speaking gigs.

Family

Irma Ehrlich persevered past her ninety-sixth birthday. Fabrics absorb memories like dye. We treasure the frothy ivory lace gown she wore when she married Erwin and the dirndl she wore when hiking Alpine meadows. Her grandchildren and great-grandchildren share gems of family lore.

Jakob Ehrlich was the first prominent Austrian to die at Dachau. Viennese Jews set up the Jakob Ehrlich Society in London in his honor and named a B'nai B'rith chapter in Tel Aviv for him in 1950. In 1988, Vienna erected a plaque at City Hall for Jakob and other Jewish statesmen murdered for their prominence. His commemorative stone outside the apartment at 22 Weimarer Street was placed in 2008. He is buried at Zentralfriedhof Cemetery Gate 4 Section 8A Row 1 Number 9.

Johann and Karla Hütter, Irma's parents, wrote loving notes in tiny script under censored conditions after Nazis drove them from their home. Karla died at Terezín in 1942 at age seventy-two, possibly of typhus. Johann was sent on to Treblinka in October of 1942, where he was murdered. Among the Hütters, Johann's sister Mary's descendants still live in the US, and one Hütter cousin, Otto, survived.

Edna and Friedrich (Fritz) Werner, Irma's sister and her husband, were deported to Terezín. Both died after deportation to Auschwitz. Their children, Lilly, Hannah, and John Werner survived the war through Irma's intervention. John remained in England. Lilly moved to Brazil with her husband; Hannah moved to Israel. Irma's other sister, Mela Brok, died in childbirth in 1922, and her two boys died—Heini, before the war, of diphtheria; and Rudi as a fighter in the Warsaw Ghetto Uprising.

Moritz and Julie [Julia] Singer, Irma's grandparents, lie buried together in the Jewish cemetery at Klatovy. After Moritz died at sixty-seven, Julie lived on to the age of eighty-four with family in České Budějovice. Both died before the Holocaust. Offspring Rudolf, Siegmund, and Louise fared well in America after arrival in the 1870s and 1880s.

Ernst and Paul Singer, Paul's cousins, found illegal passage to Palestine in 1940 and were refused entry due to their lack of visas. They were among those loaded onto a Mauritius-bound ocean liner called the SS *Patria.* Jewish activists planted a bomb to try to prevent it from sailing. Ernst and Paul survived the bomb, swam ashore, and remade their lives in Israel.

Friends

Magda Klinger was Irma's feisty classmate in Budějovice who claimed she was exempt from behaving like a proper German girl because she was a Zionist. She emigrated to Palestine as a pioneer in a kibbutz.

Leo Knook was the Dutch hiker converted away from Nazi sympathies by Irma. He tried to help Irma in Vienna and during their flight to London. Late in the war, his fiancé wrote to Irma that he had been killed in the bombing of Rotterdam.

Rosa and Sylvester Mazura were staunchly anti-Nazi Czech Catholics who lived downstairs from the Ehrlich family at 22 Weimarer Street and saved Irma's belongings. Their quiet heroism is celebrated also in Julie Metz's 2021 book, *Eva and Eve,* about her mother's childhood in the same building. The Mazuras visited Jakob's grave at the Jewish cemetery on All Saints' Day, and Rosa sent beloved recipes to Irma in New York.

Klara Taschek, Irma's girlhood friend and daughter of the Catholic mayor of Budějovice, secretly harbored the daughter of Jewish lawyer Israel Kohn (Jakob's onetime employer) in her home until the end of World War II.

Maus Westen, Irma's classmate in Budějovice, came from a German supremacist family. Her brother Hans was hanged for Nazi war crimes in 1947. The city's Nazi headquarters was at Deutsches Haus, where Irma had played Titania at sixteen. The building has become an art center under a new name.

Others whose descendants may find their way to this book include friends named **Steiner, Laster, Neubrunn, Rosenberg, Krassny, Kassner,** and **Immerglück.**

Acknowledgments

—✦———————————✦—

A thousand thanks to the people whose knowledge, judgment, and kindness influenced this book, including:

Dori Jones Yang, author, who gentled this book along from start to finish. Without her example, encouragement, mentorship, and friendship, this book would not have happened. Fact.

Doron Rabinovici, historian and author of *Eichmann's Jews*, whose informed insight helped me to interpret the meaning of Eichmann's interactions with my grandparents.

Lee Montgomery and Karalyn Ott, who steered me right during development of the manuscript with persistent nudges and removal of blockages.

Kyna Rubin, who edited, encouraged, and kibbitzed; and Barry Schumacher, whose knowledge of history added a story.

Scott Seligman, historian and author of *The Great Kosher Meat War of 1902*, who caught omissions and guided generously.

Mary Singer Wellever, who turned out to be on a first-name basis with common ancestors of 150 years ago and shared her trove of Singer family treasures. Score.

Julie Metz, author, who designed the cover with an intimate understanding of time and place based on overlapping family histories in one building in Vienna, which she wrote about in *Eva and Eve*. Julie is part of the team at She Writes Press, my esteemed publisher.

Jim Ehrlich and Julie Zdrojewski, who partnered with me in resurrecting memories of Irma, locating photographs, reviewing drafts, and celebrating the Oxford comma.

John Davis, who tolerated my fevers and furies, checked me on history and geography, and tilted at adjectives.

Contributors to *Wikipedia, Geni.com,* and the *Jewish Virtual Library*, the grand resources that help us get our stories straight.

I am grateful to all of you, and to those I have not remembered to name whose support has buoyed me through this journey.

Bibliography

Adunka, Evelyn, "Jakob und Irma Ehrlich," *Chilufim: Der Zeitschrift für Jüdische Kulturgeschicht der Universität Salzburg*, no. 2, reprinted in *Die Jüdischnationale Partei in Österreich 1906–1938*, Salzburg: Salzburg University Press, 2009, 205–08.

Albright, Madeleine, *Prague Winter: A Personal History of Remembrance and War, 1937–1948*, New York: Harper, 2012.

Arendt, Hannah, *Eichmann in Jerusalem: A Report on the Banality of Evil*, New York: Penguin, 1977.

Berkley, George E., *Vienna and Its Jews: The Tragedy of Success, 1880s–1980s*, Madison Books, 1988.

Czeike, Felix, ed. *Wien 1938: Forschungen und Beiträge zur Wiener Stadtgeschichte*, Wien: Österreichischer Bundesverlag, 1978.

de Waal, Edmund, *The Hare with Amber Eyes: A Hidden Inheritance*, London: Picador, 2011.

Frankl, Viktor E., *Man's Search for Meaning*, Boston: Beacon Press, 2006.

Freidenreich, Harriet Pass, *Jewish Politics in Vienna, 1918–1938*, Bloomington: Indiana University Press, 1991.

Fromkin, David, *A Peace to End All Peace: The Fall of the Ottoman Empire and the Creation of the Modern Middle East*, New York: Henry Holt and Company, 2009.

Gay, Peter, *My German Question: Growing Up in Nazi Berlin*, New Haven: Yale University Press, 2008.

Golabek, Mona, and Lee Cohen, *The Children of Willesden Lane: Beyond the Kindertransport: A Memoir of Music, Love, and Survival*, New York: Grand Central Publishing, 2003.

Hanna, Stan, translator, *Austria-Hungary's Last War, 1914–1918*, Volumes 1–7, Vienna: Publisher of Military Science Releases, as seen at http://www.comroestudios.com/StanHanna/.

Hašek, Jaroslav, illustrated by Josef Lada, translated by Cecil Parrott, *The Good Soldier Švejk: and His Fortunes in the World War*, London: Penguin Classics, 2005.

Herzl, Theodor, *The Jewish State*, New York: Dover, 1988.

Iggers, Wilma, *The Jews of Bohemia and Moravia: A Historical Reader*, Detroit: Wayne State University Press, 1993.

Ingrams, Doreen, *Palestine Papers: 1917–1922: Seeds of Conflict*, London: Eland Publishing, 2010.

Janner, Greville, *To Life! The Memoirs of Greville Janner, Lord Janner of Braunstone QC*, Phoenix Mill, UK: Sutton Publishing, 2006.

Jockusch, Laura, and Gabriel N. Finder, eds., *Jewish Honor Courts: Revenge, Retribution, and Reconciliation in Europe and Israel after the Holocaust*, Detroit: Wayne State University Press, 2015.

Johnson, Paul, *A History of the Jews*, London: Phoenix Press, 2013.

King, Jeremy, *Budweisers into Czechs and Germans: A Local History of Bohemian Politics, 1848–1948*, Princeton: Princeton University Press, 2005.

Krist, Martin, *Vertreibungsschicksale: Jüdische Schüler eines Wiener Gymnasiums 1938 und ihre Lebenswege*, Wien: Turia und Kant, 1999, 145

Kushner, Harold, *Who Needs God*, New York: Summit Books, 1989.

Larson, Erik: *In the Garden of Beasts: Love, Terror, and an American Family in Hitler's Berlin*, New York: Crown Publishing Group, 2011.

Masaryk, Tomáš, and Emil Ludwig, *Defender of Democracy: Masaryk of Czechoslovakia*, New York: Arno Press, 1971.

Metz, Julie, *Eva and Eve: A Search for My Mother's Lost Childhood and What a War Left Behind*, New York: Simon and Schuster, 2021.

Nadell, Pamela, *America's Jewish Women: A History from Colonial Times to Today*, New York: W.W. Norton & Company, 2020.

O'Connor, Anne-Marie, *The Lady in Gold: The Extraordinary Tale of Gustav Klimt's Masterpiece, Portrait of Adele Bloch-Bauer*, New York: Vintage Books, 2015.

Offenberger, Ilana, *The Jews of Nazi Vienna, 1938–1945: Rescue and Destruction*, London: Palgrave Macmillan, 2017.

Rabinovici, Doron, *Eichmann's Jews: The Jewish Administration of Holocaust Vienna, 1938–1945*, Cambridge: Polity Press, 2017.

Rozenblit, Marsha, *The Jews of Vienna, 1867–1914: Assimilation and Identity*, Albany: State University of New York Press, 1984.

Rozenblit, Marsha, *Reconstructing a National Identity: The Jews of Habsburg Austria during World War I*, Oxford: Oxford University Press, 2017.

Schama, Simon, *The Story of the Jews: Belonging, 1492–1900*, London: Vintage, 2018.

Tuchman, Barbara, *The Guns of August: The Outbreak of World War I*, London: Penguin Books, 2014.

Tuchman, Barbara, *The Proud Tower: A Portrait of the World Before the War, 1890–1914*, New York: Random House Trade Publishing, 2014.

Weizmann, Chaim, *Trial and Error: The Autobiography of Chaim Weizmann*, New York: Harper & Brothers Publishers, 1949.

Wistrich, Robert S., *The Jews of Vienna in the Age of Franz Joseph*, Liverpool: Littman Library of Jewish Civilization, 2006.

Zweig, Stefan, translated by Anthea Bell, *The World of Yesterday*, London: Pushkin Press, 2014.

About the Author

Catherine Ehrlich is a nonfiction writer. Trained as an Asian linguist (University of Michigan) and diplomat (Johns Hopkins SAIS), she has been a trade representative, interpreter, public relations executive, and marketing consultant in China, Hong Kong, Taiwan, and Japan as well as New York, Washington DC, and Seattle. She served as a fundraiser for the Audubon Society of Portland and is a director of the Arts Mandalay Foundation. She and her husband, John, take inspiration from nature out of home bases in Oregon and California. *Irma's Passport* is the culmination of six years of research and writing focused on the true story behind her grandmother's testimonial memoirs.

Author photo © ChrisRyanPhoto.com

SELECTED TITLES FROM SHE WRITES PRESS

She Writes Press is an independent publishing company founded to serve women writers everywhere. Visit us at www.shewritespress.com.

Quest for Eternal Sunshine: A Holocaust Survivor's Journey from Darkness to Light by Mendek Rubin and Myra Goodman. $16.95, 978-1-63152-878-1. Following the death of Mendek Rubin, a brilliant inventor who overcame the trauma of the Holocaust to live a truly joyous life, his daughter Myra found an unfinished manuscript about his healing journey; this inspirational book is that manuscript, with the missing parts of Mendek's story—along with his wisdom and secrets to finding happiness—woven in by Myra.

When a Toy Dog Became a Wolf and the Moon Broke Curfew: A Memoir by Hendrika de Vries. $16.95, 978-1631526589. Hendrika is "Daddy's little girl," but when Nazis occupy Amsterdam and her father is deported to a POW labor camp, she must bond with her mother—who joins the Resistance after her husband's deportation—and learn about female strength in order to discover the strong woman she can become.

At the Narrow Waist of the World: A Memoir by Marlena Maduro Baraf. $16.95, 978-1-63152-588-9. In this lush and vivid coming-of-age memoir about a mother's mental illness and the healing power of a loving Jewish and Hispanic extended family, young Marlena must pull away from her mother, leave her Panama home, and navigate the transition to an American world.

Prohibition Wine: A True Story of One Woman's Daring in Twentieth-Century America by Marian Leah Knapp. $16.95, 978-1-64742-061-1. When Rebecca Goldberg, a poor young widow with six children living in 1920s rural Massachusetts, had to decide between taking her older kids out of school to send them to work and breaking the law by selling illegal alcohol during Prohibition, her choice was clear: she broke the law.

Jumping Over Shadows: A Memoir by Annette Gendler. $16.95, 978-1-63152-170-6. Like her great-aunt Resi, Annette Gendler, a German, fell in love with a Jewish man—but unlike her aunt, whose marriage was destroyed by "the Nazi times," Gendler found a way to make her impossible love survive.